C000063475

Average
Mohamed

Average Mohamed

Mohamed

Freedom Fighter

Mohamed Ahmed

PALMETTO
PUBLISHING

Charleston, SC
www.PalmettoPublishing.com

Average Mohamed
Copyright © 2022 by Mohamed Ahmed

All rights reserved

No portion of this book may be reproduced, stored in a retrieval system, or transmitted in any form by any means—electronic, mechanical, photocopy, recording, or other—except for brief quotations in printed reviews, without prior permission of the author.

Hardcover ISBN: 979-8-8229-0537-5
Paperback ISBN: 979-8-8229-0928-1
eBook ISBN: 979-8-8229-0929-8

Table of Contents

Chapter 1
The Reasoning

Who, What, Where, Why, and What to Do

Hi, I am Average Mohamed. Who is Average Mohamed? This is the true story of how I became a global activist in the fight against hate, extremism, and in the cause of democracy. Let me start with what led to Average Mohamed becoming a freedom fighter.

The year was 2014. Unless you live under a rock, you are aware of the outcomes of violent jihadist movements' recruitment activities around the world.

I live in the great state of Minnesota. Being biased, I call it the greatest state in America. You must know Minnesota to understand why I call it the greatest place for me on earth.

In 1990 George H. W. Bush sent our noble soldiers to Somalia in Operation Restore Hope. He sent our marines, navy, air force, and army into harm's way to stop what amounted to a biblical-style mass starvation after food was weaponized by warlords across the country. The nation of Somalia disintegrated into factions of tribes led by soldiers and mutineers who robbed, killed, raped, and starved their nation because of their tribal affiliations.

I was lucky to have grown up in Kenya, on an island off the coast of the Indian Ocean, in a town called Mombasa. It has been a city for over one thousand years, a cosmopolitan society where our neighbors

1

were Indians, Africans, and even a Canadian missionary, meaning a white family.

My cousin in America, a woman, joined the marines as a translator. Marines who came to Kenya from Somalia for rest and relaxation often visited the house where I grew up. I fell in love with the marines then and have been a marine fanatic ever since.

In that same year, President Bush gave refugee status—later reaffirmed by President Bill Clinton—to Somalis to allow them to come to America. In a war, the ones who leave first are those with the means to get out. It starts with the rich, the intelligentsia, and the middle class, and the last to leave are usually the poor.

That trajectory of immigration has been true for those coming to America from Somalia. It was the rich who came first, then the intelligentsia, those that worked in government and other professional capacities: the lawyers, doctors, teachers, and even engineers. Then came the middle class, who could bribe a *Mukalla's*, or what Americans call a "coyote," to sneak them into America or Europe from Africa.

What kicked in next was the formalization of immigration directly from refugee camps in Africa to America. This process was in full swing by 1995, and thousands of Somalis were relocating to America. This has been the history of America from the British voyage on the Mayflower to today's Boeing 747 bringing refugees into the greatest country in the world.

One of the first flights that came into America for new Somali refugees was flight number 13 from Kenya. Hence, the new Somali immigrants were called Flight 13 by those who had been settled in America since 1900, when some had come to New York as sailors and spread across the East Coast of America. It was a derogatory term used to divide two distinct classes: the settled Somali by 1995 to the newly arrived refugee, fresh off the boat or, in this instance, plane.

The refugee resettlement program designated, California; New York; Atlanta, Georgia; Virginia, and Minnesota as suitable places to settle the new Somali community. Many other states accepted Somalis as refugees in relocations. These were the Clinton years of governance.

The economy was booming; peace was at hand. The demise of our archenemy, the Bolsheviks, had happened, and in America the good times were here.

I was a youth then, in my teens. The most important aspect of America to me was my contact with the marines, these young, idealistic kids who came halfway across the world to do good on behalf of humanity. The second most important contact was with the culture of America: Black Entertainment Television and Music Television, known by the acronyms BET and MTV. Hollywood reigned supreme in the export of American culture. I wanted badly to come to America. In the mid-1990s, I did. The very first Sunday I was here, I was to watch American football, another passion I would pick up. The Super Bowl itself. I grew up playing rugby, so this was new, like driving on the left side after coming from British system of driving on the right side. Everything was new, but I remember the good parts.

The things you remember are rather unique: the first Sunday in America, watching the Chargers play and win the Super Bowl. I don't recall the score of the game, but I vividly recall eating Doritos nachos with cheese for the first time. The taste and uniqueness were unbelievable. This was a harbinger for me of things to come in America.

I was in Houston, Texas, then moved to Virginia and started school at George Mason University, where I spent most of my time in fraternity party houses rather than classes. Everything was a heady, new exploration for me. By 1998, my sister had gotten married and moved to Minnesota. All I can recall is the Vikings losing to Atlanta in the playoffs. But when I landed in Minnesota, coming from Dulles International Airport in Washington, D.C., to Minneapolis-Saint Paul International Airport, I was picked up by a cab with a Somali driver. At the hotel where I was staying, everyone from the front desk to the cleaners of the rooms and the doorman were Somali. I went to a mosque and heard a sermon in Somali, then ate, in a Somali restaurant, my favorite dish, injera and Ber, a flat wrap made of eggs, flour, and oil with sautéed liver, cooked to a crisp. I knew then that I had found my home away from home and didn't even go back to pack my stuff to move from Virginia to Minnesota.

Life here was odd jobs. I tried going back to school at the University of Minnesota to get a degree. I successfully failed out because I spent most of my time having fun rather than being serious about my education and goals. Apparently, most Somalis figured out the same thing I did in Minnesota: that it is our community's home away from home. Most didn't speak English, but you could get a decent job that paid well as an unskilled worker in America. This was before NAFTA killed it all and shipped the jobs across our borders, where employers could find unskilled workers cheaper and with less regulations. This was the 1990s heading into the 2000s, good times in America. I had landed in Minnesota, and by the end of the week, I had lined up two jobs, both paying above minimum wage, as a customer service representative in odd jobs for corporate America. Word had gone out in our community: come work at the turkey factories and get paid very well. It didn't hurt that Minnesota was generous in its welfare system. That Catholic charities, Jewish organizations, and even Lutheran social services would help in the resettlement process of adapting to America. What we didn't tell each other was how cold Minnesota was. The first Flight 13 folks figured that one out quickly, with frostbite being common. But like the musician Prince, a native of Minnesota, said, the cold keeps the bad people out. This is what I told myself, coming from an island to the frozen American North.

Minnesota has a motto: "The Land of 10,000 Lakes." But its true name is "Minnesota nice." The people who settled here were Native Americans: the Ojibwe, Lakota, Dakota, Mdewakanton, and other tribes. Then came the Northern Europeans: the Norwegians, Swedes, Finns, Poles, and Serbians. Then came the Irish and the African Americans. In the 1970s, after the Vietnam War, the Vietnamese and the Hmong people came to Minnesota just like the Somalis had in the '90s. Today we have Afghans and Ukrainians coming into Minnesota. You must understand that our heritage of being nice comes from these peoples, who decided to be nice to one another, to care for one another,

4

to provide for one another and build a society for one another. A welcoming society that is open to all.

I'm not saying there are not deficiencies here and there, some glaring, such as the economics of color. But here, at least, one can achieve, dream, and, if you are willing to work for it, get it. The people are just nice. I investigated it. I lived in the South and spent my youth traveling the breadth of this country in pursuit of tail, fun, and adventure, sleeping on couches from Texas to Louisiana, New York to Massachusetts, Georgia to Tennessee, Ohio to Pennsylvania. Every city and state have its rhythms and dispositions, from loud New York to the sultry South. But Minnesota is a soft-spoken state of clean language with a persona that is welcoming to all, especially in my beloved city of Minneapolis. As my friend, the former police chief of Saint Paul, reminds me as a gibe, Saint Paul is mentioned in the Bible, not Minneapolis.

Here I settled; I found income and a living, and the rest of my family joined us in Minnesota. I found love, got married, and had four kids. I bought my first house and got loans to buy cars. In essence, I got my American dream of self-sufficiency, all because Minnesota is the greatest state to call home. Here all things are possible. Nothing limits you but your ingenuity and hard work.

Who? Al-Shabab, ISIS, and al-Qaeda Came to Town

When 2001 rolled around, the good times were upended by the coming of a new enemy. Violent jihadis call them the Magnificent 19. Patriot Day happened on September 11. On that day, over three thousand of citizens of the world, not just Americans, were murdered in cold blood. Thousands more died from toxic-waste exposure from the site. Even today, decades later, folks are still dying from that day's events.

Here were nineteen individuals who, like me, had come to America, an open society that not only welcomed them but even trained them in flying planes. They were led by a guy named Mohamed Atta, named, like me, after the greatest human being to have lived on this planet, the Prophet Muhammad, peace be upon him, who our parents wanted us to follow. Here these nineteen came, all men, all foreign like me, all welcomed like me. But unlike me, they chose to harm, kill, and murder on a grand scale in America.

That was the end of peace as we knew it in America, which assumed a war footing to try deal with this menace, now that what used to defend America from harm—two seas, Pacific and Atlantic—no longer sufficed. Think about this: the last time the American homeland was attacked was in the War of 1812. Through World Wars I and II, the mutually assured nuclear destruction by the Bolsheviks of the USSR, the Vietnam War, and even the Gulf War, the American homeland remained untouched and unmolested. Then came nineteen men armed with razors, taking over planes and smashing into our heroes at the Pentagon and the Twin Towers of New York, killing not only themselves but also civilian women, men, and children in a mass murder. These nineteen were led by men who called their organization the Base, or al-Qaeda in Arabic, led by Osama bin Laden and Dr. Ayman al-Zawahiri.

We didn't know what to make of this as Muslims in America. Here we were, building, working, and living the greatest of lives in America, free as birds in the greatest country built on ideals of freedom, liberty, and rights for all. Well, mostly all. And we woke up to Islamophobia on September 12 because of the death cult of al-Qaeda. Suddenly, young Muslim men were threats in America. One thing I loved about George W. Bush was his attempt to distance Islam and majority Muslims from this phenomenon of terrorism. He walked into a mosque to send that message. Until that moment, no other American president had walked into a mosque to deliver a message to leave Muslims alone. That was one reason why I became a Republican.

But I digress. We continued living our lives, but things were never the same again. Gone was the innocence of our Somali American, and even Muslim American, community in America. Now we were all suspects. Watching the media, especially from the right, the left was no better; they trumpeted our communities as the fifth column of an impending invasion in America. Hysteria, misinformation, and the beat of war took over the country. We went to war justly in Afghanistan to clear out al-Qaeda and those who gave them sanctuary, the Taliban. They were two groups of the same feather, violent extremists who believed in the mass murder of others to achieve political ends. Then we went to war in Iraq to clear out a dictator who was a thorn in our you-know-what when it came to regional hegemony and American foreign-policy goals. Two Muslim countries were—well, we said "liberated," but it amounted to an occupation. We went to save them, as it was sold to the public then, but neither country wanted us to save them—or even to save themselves, as we have learned in hindsight, after losing $6 trillion in treasure and the most important commodity we have in America, the blood of our soldiers, spies, diplomats, and aid-workers of mercy.

We, especially I, continued to live life in pursuit of the American dream. By 2007 an affiliate of al-Qaeda popped up in Somalia. It was called al-Shabab, meaning "the Youth." Let me go back to its origins first. When George H. W. Bush sent American soldiers into Somalia, al-Qaeda sent its soldiers into Somalia. You must have heard of the "Black Hawk Down" story, when American Black Hawk helicopters were shot down in Mogadishu and dead American soldiers were dragged in the streets. We later learned that al-Qaeda's bin Laden, at that time in Sudan, had sent trainers to teach and act out the attack. This was in 1993. By 2001 a new group of Somali violent jihadists affiliated with Al Qaeda, which was called al-Ittihad in Somalia, had developed a quasi-militia and government in Mogadishu. It was called the Islamic Courts Union. People hated the warlords then; their butchery and disrepute had alienated even the tribes, with their constant warring, rapes, looting and mayhem. These same groups were used clandestinely by American intelligence, which helped the warlords track down wanted foreign nationals who were known al-Qaeda affiliates in Somalia. Apparently, the Islamic Courts Union harbored elements of the core of al-Qaeda in Somalia.

What did America do? Never a good student of history, America, along with Europe, subcontracted the process of clearing the Islamic Courts Union to Somalia's neighbors, the Ethiopians. The international community, led by America, was cobbling together a semblance of governance based on democracy for Somalia. This government was a government on paper. Regional states had formed independently, and others were controlled by warlords or violent jihadists—including Mogadishu, which was controlled by the Islamic Courts Union. The people loved the Islamic Courts Union, for it brought peace, order, and responsible governance to Mogadishu and surrounding areas, compared to the warlords who were backed by the West and neighboring countries. The ultimate irony of history is that Somalis have been fighting Ethiopians over land and resources in the region since the seventh century. As late as 1977, Somalis fought a war that they lost against Ethiopia, thanks to Bolsheviks and Cuban mercenaries on the Ethiopian side. It doesn't take a genius to figure out what Somalis will do when they learn the Ethiopians have crossed the border into Somalia. The Ethiopians did as they were supposed to do for their interests and those of the West: they cleared the Mogadishu area of the Islamic Courts Union. Then the Islamists who wanted governance and the affiliated warlords defected to the government. Those already with al-Qaeda formed al-Shabab, "the Youth Movement." At first, they didn't advertise that they were al-Qaeda. They presented themselves as a nationalist movement in opposition to the Ethiopian occupation. By 2007 this issue had found ready recruits here in Minnesota to join al-Shabab. Some youths left America—Somali kids, boys, and girls—to join the war effort.

As a community, we were not surprised. I mean that we understood the underlying factors. Unchecked nationalism is a potent draw. We were Somalis. Al-Shabab at that time was not al-Qaeda, not in a full-blown or publicly understood way, but the US government knew quite well that there were al-Qaeda elements in the hierarchy of the organization that had to be destroyed for the national security of America. But I don't mean to say we were not shocked. What really shocked us was kids leaving to join the Islamic State of Iraq and Syria (ISIS) in 2014.

What? 2014 Youths Leaving

In 2014 the Islamic State came to our towns in Minnesota. They targeted our Somali American community and Muslims across the world for recruitment. Our youths joining in with the Islamic State to go to Iraq and Syria shocked us to the core. I mean, going back to Somalia is one thing; we are Somalis, and Somalia is the motherland. But Iraq and Syria? That was the moment we said, OK, we have a serious problem in our Muslim communities. Of course, this was a national security issue. But we could not understand why our youths, who were blessed to live in America, the greatest country in the world, would want to leave. Why would our youths want to leave our democracy, where we get to choose our leaders by our rights, freedoms, and liberties? Where we have access to health care, education, and work, and to dignity that comes from them? Where, despite some misgivings, life is good compared to in Somalia, or even to Iraq or Syria, at war at that time? We came as refugees and immigrants by our own self-cognition and choice to raise our kids in this land of the free and the brave, where dreams of a good life are almost possible if one exerts oneself and plays by the rules of our laws and our awesome Constitution. We, the first generation, did not get it. This was a taboo subject among our community. Most of us chose to continue the pursuit of our own happiness, but this bothered me to no end.

The issue then hit close to home. My niece, who I will not name out of respect for her family here in America, left to go to Iraq and landed in Syria. She had lived in Saint Paul, a good girl with no gang affiliation. She did well and was never a nuisance. A perfect student who wanted to be a nurse, she helped raise her siblings. She stole a passport and left, going through many countries. She had saved up some money and landed in Raqqa, Syria, where she called her family to say, "I have joined my real family." Imagine that. We Somalis are thick in bloodlines. To abandon one's family for another ideal is considered the worst of attributes by our people. Imagine believing the idea that your family is not moral, and your country is evil when the cause you joined commits murder and mayhem in the name of a false ideology carried by a death cult calling itself the most noble of names, the Islamic State. Why did my niece leave our democracy, our republic, and our society, leaving behind a distraught family, to put herself in harm's way in Raqqa in the middle of a civil war between the butchers of Syria, whether the Islamists or the secular Ba'athist dictator? I did not get it, but this and other incidents of kids leaving Minnesota shocked our community to the core. We were ashamed, alarmed, and at the same time embarrassed by what they did. We are just like other Americans; we did not understand it and the issues that led these youths, our kids, to leave.

Now, I am a curious human being. I question things to understand them. So I did what naturally comes to me. I went to my cousin's house to find out what had happened here. I sat down with my cousin and asked, "How could you not see what was happening to your daughter?"

She said, "My daughter helped me raise my children. She was a responsible and loving daughter. She had no bad habits I could think of, but like the youths of this generation, she used her phone a lot. Because I saw nothing wrong happening, I let that independence develop in her. She helped me navigate society in America. She understood the system here better than I did. She was my guide and my hope."

She then looked at us, together there with a friend. She asked, "What is social media?" The FBI had come to her house and told her that her daughter had been recruited through social media accounts. She had texted back to her mother from Syria that she is what she wanted to become: a nurse in Raqqa, Syria. The anguish in the mother is palpable.

She said to us, "When a child dies, you *sabr*. Have patience because the child went back to God—'from God we come, to God we go back,' we say as Muslims. But what does a parent do when your child is in harm's way across the world and cannot come back after alienating her country, which gave us a home and rights, and you don't want her to stay there? How does a mother sleep a full night without worries and pain in her heart?"

I went home and cried. I cried because my niece was in harm's way because of her own decisions. An eighteen-year-old who chose to leave us and put my cousin in permanent pain and anguish. We in the mainstream are worried about the impact of these youths leaving; we Muslims worry about not only that but the impact it has on the families who were abandoned for life in a death cult like al-Shabab, al-Qaeda, or ISIS. In the end, Minnesota became the most prolific contributor of violent jihadists leaving America. There was no known profile of the kids who joined the death cults of al-Shabab, al-Qaeda, or ISIS. They were ex-gang members, honorary valedictorian students, college students, high school students, Somalis. They were black, Arab, white, middle-class, rich, new converts, reverts, and even drug users. The FBI spent money to try to figure out a profile of these kids who were joining in with violent jihadis. FBI Director James Comey is on record as saying there is no known profile of a person joining a terrorist group—not one defining issue. Myriad issues and complex answers came back to them from research that stated clearly that it could be anyone, with a combination of factors. The factors are as many as the sand along the seashore. There is no known profile.

This piqued my mind. Curiosity got the best of me. I began my own detailed research into the causes of the violent jihadist. What is it about this ideology that is taking our kids from our beloved America? Lord knows it did not make sense to me, and at that time, it did not make sense to our governments, either, across the world. It was not just America; by the end of the war in Iraq and Syria, it is estimated that over forty thousand volunteers had left the global countries to join the Islamic State in Iraq and Syria. That is forty thousand who left the Americas, Europe, the Middle East, Africa, Asia, and Australia. No country in the world can claim that their citizens did not join in to go kill and murder in Syria or Iraq in the last several decades.

Governments were perplexed by this. They, like our community in Minnesota, just did not get it. How could they? Who joins in with killers and butchers of humanity? How are we to understand that being worried about things in the world that are daily needs? Things like health care, education, shelter, standards of living, and taxes—oh, taxes and more taxes—while earning something to put it all together? The daily grind of life. Governments are worried about law and order, creating systems of viability and mobility, with safety in mind for most if not all. How could we understand joining a group that wants to dismantle this order for an order built on skulls, bones, and the blood of others by submission to their will through terror? How does one even begin doing research into this issue? Again, my curiosity got the best of me. So I started with the best of sources: open media. What is the vanguard of democracy, the free press, saying about this issue? I got disgusted because the blame-Islam crowd was in full swing in American media. I started reading international media done by ethnic communities and independent sources. The freelancers who delve deep into the issue. The ones that go beyond sound bites.

Why? Propaganda Was Effective

What I learned from my research is this: The al-Shabab, al-Qaeda, and ISIS propaganda directed at our youths works. *Works.* It is effective and research based. but designed to appeal and convince others of the justness of their cause.

Let me start with my first insight. Now, I am in no terms an expert, just an Average Mohamed looking at the information I perused between work, home, and living over time. The very first thing I realized is how the propaganda appropriated Islam's holiest of holy terminology.

Let's start with the concept of jihad. What is jihad? It means "struggle." Struggle in the path of God. There are two types of jihads. If you ask any true-believing Muslim, "Are you a jihadist?" a true believer will say yes. The first jihad, the greater jihad, is between you and your soul—*nafs*, as we call it in Islam. The struggle between your dark side and good side. The side of sin versus the side of *thawab*, good deeds. All souls struggle with this aspect; it is not unique to Islamic understanding. Even in Asia they talk of yin and yang: light and darkness, represented in two spirals of dark entwined with light. The Hindus call it karma, that doing good gets good and bad gets bad. Christians and Jews—believers in the Abrahamic tradition of one God, just like Muslims but though a different understanding—believe the greatest struggle is between your good and your bad, in essence, the struggle for your soul.

In Islam, the Prophet Muhammad, peace be upon him, taught us that the greatest struggle or jihad we have is with ourselves, our *nafs*. The *hadith*, or the sayings of the Prophet Muhammad, peace be upon him, say the following.

Once, a group of soldiers for Islam came back from a battle, and the prophet said, "You have come back from the 'lesser jihad' to the 'greater Jihad.'"

The fighters asked, "What is the greater jihad?"

Mohammad, peace be upon him, answered, "It is struggle against one's passions."

The passions are your own soul. The Soul wants more and does more but regulating to avoid mishap, to not do bad even when one can get away with it. To always do good even when others do not see, to seek solace in harmony with self, humanity, and your lord. This is the greater jihad. Every Muslim, if not all believers in a deity, will say they are in a jihad with their soul to do good and win. Call it karma, kismet, yin and yang, the laws of nature, or whatever you desire.

The second jihad is the act of war. But then again, there are stipulations of war. You are commanded in Islam to defend your home, your neighborhood, your city, your country, and the world of Islam. "Defensive" means of defending what yours or ours as Muslims. If other attacks that, then it is binding and legal to defend it. I read the United Nations charter of self-defense for nations. It says the same thing. Depending on which school of Islamic theology you belong to, they also say offensive Jihad is acceptable if commanded by legitimate political leaders. Here, the emphasis is on *legitimate political leaders*. If a country is hostile about to attack you, you are allowed to strike to defend yourself by the guidance of political leaders who are legitimate.

Who made Osama bin Laden, the head of al-Qaeda, a legitimate leader in Islam, or Abu Bakr al-Baghdadi the leader of the Islamic State? Both are now deceased, taken out by America. Maybe a community of desperate, misguided men and women chose them, but no tribe, no nations did. Their legitimacy came from the barrel of a gun, from suicide bombings and beheadings. They killed men, women, and children with their call for offensive jihad. There exist leaders, national heads in the world, who were chosen as kings or tribal heads, either democratically elected or nominated through representative means, that have the legitimacy of the people. Average Mohamed prefers democratically elected ones because the actual people chose them with respect to minority rights.

The second most important, potent detail of their propaganda is the appropriation of the term *mujahid*, which means one who struggles for the cause of Allah *subhanahu wa ta'ala*. This term is powerful because all Muslims believe they will endure for the cause of Allah *subhanahu wa ta'ala*.

What is the cause? To fight against injustice is the cause of Allah *subhanahu wa ta'ala*. To fight poverty and ignorance is the cause of Allah *subhanahu wa ta'ala*. But to fight against the enemies of God, who infringe on the people of God, is the cause of the mujahid. In essence, anybody with a rudimentary understanding of Islamic history—or even of the Quran or the *hadith*, the sayings of the Prophet Mohammad, peace be upon him—knows and understands that the mujahid is the ultimate Muslim. One who is guaranteed heaven upon demise in this world. The Quran says that though we may think they are dead, indeed, they are alive. Those who become *shahids* or die on the path and in the battles of God. This, in Islam, is what Christians call a just-war ideology. Every faith from Christianity to Hinduism to Judaism has heroes and battles that it commemorates. Islam is glorious that way, too, and the highest of designations is for those who fight in jihad and die from it. The term *mujahid* is powerful. The extremists appropriated this terminology, leaning on the teachings of jihad as the motivation of their cause. Those who caused mayhem and the random bloodshed of women, men, and children were now called *mujahid* by the extremists.

The third most important aspect is the revolutionary nature of what the terrorist is trying to do. An example is ISIS, which basically combined two states, Syria, and Iraq, destroying a border made by the colonialist Sykes-Picot Agreement. The destruction of the old-world order, which was based on a Western understanding, made way for one based on an Islamic understanding that came from Muslims, though they were terrorists. Some in the world have been chafing for centuries under the auspices and control of the Western hegemony. Not that it is all bad, but no one likes their destiny to be decided by others. Hence the revolutionary tendency to want to change things to bring in a new world order, although one that is not defined, is an attractive proposition for youths, including white kids, who want a cause and a reason for being. In essence, the West stopped giving ideas to revolutionary means of self-empowerment because society had achieved what it most desired: a comfortable way of life. The discomfort of bringing about a new system, though ill-defined, made by the bones and blood of others though not told that way, but idealists tag on to them. Comfort of the western society leads to malaise that revolutionaries find easy recruits for those idealistic enough to want change of their order. They recruits saw themselves as the lot who were bringing in a new world order. The extremists claim it will be built on Islam. There's nothing wrong with Islam being a viable system of governance, but the *how* is what shocks the world. The butchery, the beheadings, the public executions, the suicide bombings, the stoning, and other means of terror are not in sync with our age today. Majority Muslims revolt at extremism, but extremists do not need a majority to pull off a revolution. They need a few diehard believers in the cause, and the cause is revolutionary compared to the demands of a youth in the West. The demands on youth are easy in the West. Access to everything and a good life if you play by the rules and laws equally applies to all. You can live a comfortable life. The youths for whom extremism is appealing don't see that; they see the pull of their newfound struggle as a revolution they want to take part in.

What is the revolution? A good example is ISIS calling itself a caliphate. Abu Bakr al-Baghdadi called himself a caliph. Now, every Muslim believes in the caliphates, which depend on your *madhab*, your sect or school of thought. For majority Muslims who are Sunni, there are four recognized caliphs in the history of early Islam: Abu Bakr, Uthman, Omar, and Ali, *radhialhu anhum*, the known companions of the Prophet Mohammad, peace be upon him. These four are universally recognized caliphs of the Muslim world. Every leader who came after them claimed that mantle, some legitimately, most illegitimately. Abu Bakr al-Baghdadi claimed he was a caliph, and the Islamic State was a caliphate, one in which all Muslims were duty-bound to pay oaths of allegiance. This was powerful messaging as a strategy to get recruits to join in their revolution. Abu Bakr al-Baghdadi carved up Syria and Iraq and called Raqqa, Syria, the capital of his caliphate. From across the world came the loyalty oaths of insurgents and terrorists interested in forming an alliance. From there came the volunteers. While majority Muslims in the world shunned and were appalled by ISIS, claiming the caliphate was a Cali-fake, some youths found this formation of the caliphate to be historical and an opportunity to bring back what had existed before, a true revolution, not knowing that this was not a caliphate but a Cali-fake built by murderers and butchers with no souls to speak of, with death as the reward of membership, for its followers and the public who ended up under their domain.

The last reason I found the propaganda of extremists to be appealing is the disjointing of the global system. These are issues pertaining to new global trade imbalances and political power being limited to those with means. This is how it has always been, but in this age, with the demise of work in the towns, cities, and states of the West, it is glaringly so. Once, one could work a lifetime for three generations in factories or industries, but the pay is far less now, and the jobs are being shipped out to cheaper, smarter labor populations across the world. In this society, the dreams of many matters less than the dreams of the few, who pinch ever more astronomical profits from the masses.

There's nothing wrong with capitalism. But from the 2000s until recently, and especially around 2014, some of the unemployed, uninspired, idealistic Muslim youth of the world found solace in the destruction of the current global order. Where you find unemployment, you will find violent jihadists; where you find poverty binding the people, you will find violent jihadists; where you find great inequities in society, such as racism, Islamophobia, and the hatred of others, you will find violent jihadists. But the same is true of anarchists, communists, right-wingers, and hate groups of the racial kind and the far left, like antifa, or domestic terrorism groups.

In my research on violent jihadists, I found this to be true in Europe, America, Canada, Asia, and Africa. Wherever Muslims were marginalized and put into different societies—independent and poor, like ghettos—Islamists who advocated for violence found a ready-made supply of alienated youths who were willing to hear alternatives to their lives because things sucked for them as they were. Where injustice reigned supreme, the violent jihadist offered violence as the cure. For some who were fed up with injustice in their state, society, or community, this was appealing—a way out. The Islamic State was offering houses, cars, armories, sex slaves, and even stipends to those who moved to them. Imagine an unemployed, disenfranchised youth anywhere in the world hearing that; they will move.

What they didn't tell them was that these houses, cars, and even weapons were appropriated from Yazidis, Christians, Jews, moderate Muslims, and the state government through brutality, rape, murder, and mayhem, which, when they joined, these youths had to continue to do or cause. to keep what they had gotten from the extremists. This was not Islam but thuggery, butchery, and thieving on a grand scale. This appealed to those who wanted a new order by creating chaos in the old-world order of peace, laws, and customs that respected human dignity, rights, liberties, private property, and commerce unregulated by people's consent.

What to Do? Create Counter-Ideology

This, by all accounts, is an average assessment. Again, I remind you all that I successfully failed in pursuit of higher learning, but I came to understand that these are the core issues. I ask you, as you read, to understand that I am just an Average Mohamed. Not Scholar Mohamed, not Doctor Mohamed, not Social Scientist Mohamed, but just like you. A common man trying to figure out a problem the world has faced, using a layman's means of understanding. By now you understand that I am big on talking plainly and straightforward in my assessments. This is my superpower. I don't go deep into the weeds like the smart people who claim that to understand what they say you have to have a PhD. I simply state what I know, the details I know, and tell you straightforwardly. I am just a regular guy trying to figure things out. I could be wrong, but research and history have proven me right. That is a rare thing for me because I am often wrong in my understanding, but I am willing to learn to understand and be better. So please, if I'm wrong, excuse me, but even better, reach out and educate me. I am always eager and curious to learn. The best learning is unsolicited and comes from others.

The next question I had was, *what can I do?* I mean, I figured out some stuff above, but what can an actual Average Mohamed do about it? The options in America did not appeal to me. Like find work in our government to help cause against violent Jihadists for a capitalist like me an anathema to making means they pay them less than I wanted or join. How about becoming a noble American soldier for a guy who can't do ten push-ups or even survive boot camp, those options were out as possibilities for me. This issue was a conundrum for me. I understood that the propaganda was having an effect in my community, recruiting kids from my beloved Minnesota in our homeland, the great America. But what could I do about it? What would you do?

I spent a month thinking about this while going to work at my store, which I owned. I hit upon an article that described the propagandists making the messages disseminated by al-Qaeda and ISIS. They were regular folks. Nothing special. Not imams or PhD students or rich folks or even government-sponsored individuals. They were just regular folks. Why is it they had the conviction we lacked here in America, which the world needed to counter them?

Fear was one major factor; resource allocation was another. More important, who wants the hustle of dealing with issues of global complexity when the daily grind of life is complex enough already? I remembered a speech by a Catholic guy; one thing about me is that I watch and read a lot of history and love history. This age of ours in the West, this me-me-me culture, is not what I aspired to be. Do not get me wrong: I am a vain me-me-me person too. But I also see we-we-we, the people aspect of things. That is me, too, a conundrum that compartmentalizes the issues of "me" and "we, the people."

This Catholic guy was speaking during his inauguration. In that speech he said the following: "Ask not what your country can do for you—ask what you can do for your country." His name, you may know, was John F. Kennedy. An idealistic president, one I dare call a lion because he understood one factor. His greatest asset was the American people.

There is more to that speech. He also said, "Hold us accountable." Imagine that—a powerful man demanding we hold him and his administration accountable. This guy, who was Irish American, started the Peace Corps. Now, this is an organization that sends American youths to the poorest communities across the world to help build things, teach, or even dispense basic health care. They're just kids seeking adventure who have a revolutionary zeal and believe that America is here to help the downtrodden of the world.

As for why I call Kennedy a lion, you see, my grandfather taught my father, who taught me, an African fable. The lion cried, perched on a hill, "Why do they hate me so much in this kingdom of the jungle?"

The sheep, upon hearing this lament, shouted back, "You are lucky. You get to hunt what you want, live free of fear of other animals in this kingdom, do what you want, and still cry about being hated. What about me, who gets eaten by the will of others? I would rather be hated than eaten. In essence, be a lion and let your enemies hate you for what you are. At that time, the Bolsheviks of the USSR were coming hard at America and the world of free people that followed the ways Lincoln had taught power of the people, by the people, for the people. Let them hate us, but we will do what we want in helping humanity. President Kennedy understood this when he sent the youth away in the Peace Corps, which America still does today. As Americans we do what we want for the good of humanity. That does not mean we are saints, but we aspire to those lofty goals. Let our enemies hate us, but we are lions as a people. The natives of America share the same sentiments as my grandfather and father, whom I brought to America.

"What can I do for my God, for my country, and for humanity in this instance?" I questioned myself repeatedly. I let this issue dwell in my thoughts day and night while continuing my research, which expanded into other researchers' works. This issue of violent jihadis bothered me to no end, and all available means of fighting them sounded, well, not to my taste, or just not me. I am a man of peace and nonviolence. I value law and order but within reason. I am a Somali; we are born libertarians as the nomads of this world, coming from nomads in our bloodlines. We move, live, and build wherever we lay our heads at night. We are egalitarian yet very insular as a people. We strive, as we were taught by our mothers, to be among the best. Come to our weddings, funerals, and functions and you will hear our poetry, *buraanbur* by our womenfolk and clergy prayers that talk of our bloodlines, our heritage, and our worth. We are those who consider ourselves equals among equals in this world. We are proudly Muslims. What can I do now that I am an American Muslim?

On August 4, 2014, I said the following words in public before the magistrate court among other newly minted Americans: "I hereby declare that I absolutely and entirely renounce and abjure all allegiance and fidelity to any foreign prince, potentate, state, or sovereignty of whom or which I have heretofore been a subject or citizen; that I will support and defend the Constitution and laws of the United States of America against all enemies foreign and domestic; that I will bear true faith and allegiance to the same; that I will bear arms on behalf of the United States when required by the law; that I will perform noncombatant service in the Armed Forces of the United States when required by the law; that I will perform work of national importance under civilian direction when required by the law; and that *I take this obligation freely, without any mental reservation or purpose of evasion.*"

I took my oath: the oath of allegiance to my democracy and republic. I became a citizen of America. This was a joyous occasion, which

I celebrated with my family and friends as if it were a wedding. I had come a long way to call myself an American. Five thousand miles, to be precise. At this junction in my life, I had lived here for longer than anywhere else in the world, including the motherland, Africa. I had taken much and given less back. Here was an enemy, foreign in that its ideology was foreign to America, but domestic, too, in that it recruited fellow Americans.

What can I do, then? The answer came in Jihadi John. Here was a Canadian who left Canada and became the most prolific recruiter that even presidents like Obama felt compelled to cry out to the Muslim public, "Please help us deflect this propaganda and messaging process for our youths." President Obama was the man who controlled a powerful capacity to deliver aid, harm, or even catastrophes to humanity. Though he was imbued with amazing rights and powers, here he was, asking, like President Kennedy, "What can you, Muslims of America, do for country?" I knew then that this time President Obama call, and the works of Jihadi John had just called it for me. The call to actions was what President Obama ask did for me. Counter-ideology would be my mission going forward. If Jihadi John could do ideological propaganda on behalf of evil while beheading people, an Average Mohamed, which is what I was—not Saint Mohamed but a sinner, not Educated Mohamed, not rich Mohamed, just an Average Mohamed with all the missteps and misgivings of average folks—would try answer with counter-ideology.

Hence an idea was born. The whole premise was to create an idea to defeat an idea. That became my focus. I began by registering myself as Average Mohamed, my new moniker. I was a businessman who knew nothing else but business, capitalism, selling a service or a product in return for a profit. This venture would be selling ideas to defeat an idea in return for peace and freedoms, for God, family, country, and humanity, the cornerstones of my life.

One of my guiding principles in life is that I was a square with four sides. One side is God; I am a sinner, not a saint, always in need of redemption, mercy, and forgiveness from the lord, and I call my God Allah *subhanahu wa ta'ala*. The second side is my family, who always bear with me through faults and mishaps and struggles but are loyal, as Somali families go to one another no matter what comes our way; we stick together always. The third side is country, the motherland we left, Africa, and our homeland that took us in, America, which gave us everything we asked for and demanded little in return. America gave us freedoms, liberty, rights, equality, citizenship, health care, education, shelter, and even opportunity to become better and more than what we aspired to be.

The last of the four sides is earning a living. I was a capitalist from the traditions of my father, his father, and his father, going back for generations, before the word "capitalist" was even invented. I would sell a service or a product to earn a living. These four corners defined me as a person. I am a square, and it was about time us squares revolted and started our own revolution. Mine is just that: an Average Mohamed, a freedom fighter fighting for the freedom of minds against extremists of violent jihadis who an abomination to Islam are. Islam is peace, and I intend, as an imperfect Muslim, not a saint, to stand on that. If Jihadi John can do it for their side, an Average Mohamed will have to do it for the side of democracies and republics. My new role is to furnish democracies and republics with ideas to defeat the ideas of extremism. Easier said than done.

Chapter 2
What Do I Know

Store Owner on the North Side of Minneapolis

Let me start with who am I first because the question that arises is what I knew up until then beyond cursory knowledge gained on insights from open media and researchers of extremism. What was I till then before taking on ideas to defeat an idea. In 2014 I was a gas station manager for the Super America corporation, a subsidiary of Speedway America now. Prior to that I owned a grocery store in an urban inner-city setting on the north side of Minneapolis. I had saved up my income and taken a loan from family to buy the grocery store. I loved Northside, which was predominantly an African American neighborhood. Like all inner cities, it had its share of problems, but what I learned earning a living predominantly from the African American community is that they are just like everyone else, good, and decent people. My attitude toward the community was that I would respect it and provide the best customer service available.

Now, my store was what you call a C-store. We called my corporation Qarey Inc.; the store was popularly known in the hood as Santana. The previous, original owners had called it Santana even though the sign outside of it said Janine Store. I never bothered to change it. The North High School, the Polar Bears, was a few blocks from my store. I sold groceries and clothes—hip-hop clothes and white T-shirts out—of the store. If you've ever been to a hood store, a bodega, as they call it in New York, you will understand what I mean. I made more money buying wholesale outfits from California, New York, and Illinois to sell in the store than I did selling groceries. The best part is that there were no taxes on clothes in Minnesota. This was all profit, minus a few taxes for interstate commerce. I kept a book in the store like my father did and his father when they owned stores, before they became major businessmen in trade in Africa. I brought the same concept of capitalism with a soul to my store. If I knew you to be a customer that had no money to pay for groceries or a clean T-shirt and underwear or needed a pack of cigarettes until next payday, I would write it down in the book and give you credit. Most people do this in ethnic stores, with the accounting done at the end of the week or month. I put a limit of no more than $100 in credit to an account per week or two, maybe a month. Folks thought I was crazy to even do this. You must understand that most murders in the city were happening within a thirty-block radius of my store. The existence of youths in gangs was common. Heck, they even taught me the slang and handshakes of the Gangster Disciples, the Bloods, and the Crips. They knew we were unaffiliated, just out there to make a living. They never bothered us at all. The word in the street was that we were cool; we didn't bother anybody and understood the code of the neighborhood. Respect was given no matter who you were, and from that respect came back to me and my staff. Most stores had bulletproofed windows and regulated how many customers were in the store. We did not do any of that. We put our faith in God, then the neighborhood. We gave credit to all we knew. When a mother was having money issues and needed bread and milk and eggs for her kids, we let them have them. When a working man needed cigarettes until he cashed his check next week, we let him have them. This cost me a lot in credit at times, running a cumulative tab of thousands of dollars. But word went around that we look out for folks. That bought loyalty to the store. If they had money to spend, they would spend it in the store before going elsewhere. I will amaze you by telling you 99.99 percent of the people paid us back. I had a guy go away to prison owing me $300, and when he came out, he asked for credit. I gave him another

$300. He got a job and paid me back with his first paycheck. That is love of one another—capitalism with a soul—and very profitable. We were making money that took our revenue to amazing heights until the foreclosures of the housing crash. The entire neighborhood seemed emptied out as whole blocks went into foreclosure. Learning the truth of America, the subprime mortgages were mostly sold to minorities, which bankrupted them in foreclosures, which meant traffic to the store went down to almost zero. Folks just did not have the means to survive, let alone going to spend that extra $10 to $20 a day in a hood store. Plus, Aldi opened, then Walmart. Now I was going to Costco, Sam's Club, Aldi, and Walmart to buy things to sell in my store. Who needed me in when other, bigger cheaper bus-line-available stores were opening in the neighborhood? Times were tough, so I and my financial backers decided to barely maintain the store by working ninety hours a week and paying ourselves less than minimum wage. After bills, taxes, and rent were paid, it was no longer worth it. As soon as our income went up with the rebounding the economy, we sold the store for a profit. I went to work for the competition. I found a job working in retail for Super America, starting as a supervisor based on my experience.

I loved my work as a gas station manager. I was good at what I did. Good enough to become a manager within six months and then get assigned to my own store within a year. I loved what I did, which was basically anything. Even though I was the manager, I believed in an all-hands-on deck philosophy. If the toilet needed cleaning and my paperwork or front-end work was done, I cleaned the toilets. If the garbage needed to be taken out at every pump and my workers had done so two days in a row, I took out the garbage. If I was the first to see a spill on the floor, I mopped it.

Bottom line, I am not afraid of hard work, even when a manager could easily delegate. Be the best at what you are; even take pride in it. Folks asked me, "Are you the manager?" and I said, "Yes, but also toilet cleaner and taking-out-garbage specialist too." Arrogance has no place in the profitability and equity of work. Work has its own dignity. I believed that when one paid you a dollar, you should give them a dollar and half's worth of work. I was a corporate man. I loved it. I would wake up and drive customer service, people like good service. The secret to running a retail store is simple: keep it clean; give fast service; get them in and out and smile; laugh and get to know and respect those spending their hard-earned money in your store. And these stores I managed, they paid me well enough to feed my children, clothe them, and pay for shelter, and even offered insurance for their health care. I had mentors along the way. The culture of corporate America is one in which everyone is training everyone to do their job. I am always curious. I wouldn't call myself smart but am determined to learn. I learned from the best in the organization, from district managers to area managers to the vice president to the art of profitability index and goals means.

I was good at what I did. The proof was in me being called the turnaround guy for failing, underperforming hood-based stores. I was sent from one hood store to another. I worked in the store opposite 38th and Chicago in Minneapolis, where George Floyd was martyred, in a quickly gentrifying neighborhood with bulletproof windows and panels. As soon as it was profitable and I had trained my replacement, an amazing black woman, to take the reins, I got pushed to a hood store that needed a miracle. The first day there, I did a walk-around as trained by corporate. I found needles and garbage everywhere and went inside. It looked like it had not had a deep cleaning. Neglect was evident. I turned this store around based on doing only one thing. I spent 90 percent of my time cleaning it. I focused on keeping it clean and well-stocked. That was my secret. It had four pumps. Once the neighborhood realized the store was clean, the people started coming to it. I asked corporate to offer extra security to put outside, and they hired off-duty Minneapolis police to do so. Once folks started seeing the police rather than strung-out folks mingling around the store, profitability went up.

My vice president came down to inspect my store. He asked me what I did to increase the profitability of a four-pump gas station by $142,000 in one year. I told him it was nothing but keeping it clean and safe, having awesome customer service and respecting people. The folks figured out this was not a hang-out store but a business and left us alone.

The neighborhood, an amazing mix of working-class people, Hispanics, whites, blacks, Somalis, Native Americans, and others came to the store because it was clean and safe thanks to off-duty Minneapolis police officers and the hard work of my team. The rest was simply executing corporate strategy and marketing.

I loved my job because it was easy but hard work. I value hard work. When I was nine, my father taught me, when he put me to work in a coffee factory (we had was working in sealing bags of coffee on the production line), "You are here on earth to tire your mind, body, and soul." That attitude stuck with me. I mean, he could have put me in his office to answer calls or do something more important than the menial job of factory-line worker in the factory he owned with his brothers.

Sad to say, both stores I helped work on are no longer open. Because of the George Floyd-based riots, the one at 38th and Chicago and the one at Bloomington and 24th, both in South Minneapolis, have shut down. I was a businessman, a corporate man, so what did I know of counter-ideology? Nothing. But I was determined to create it one way or another.

Started with Posters—That Did Not Work

Where do I start; with what do I start? I saw a poster advertising a product and thought that maybe a poster was what I needed. What kind of posters, then? What design or process do they have? I had no idea. I looked at cause-based posters. Nothing seemed to fit the bill of what I was looking for. I did not know how to make a poster. I sought out freelancers who could help. I told them of my concept, and what they produced was too Western based. I was searching for Islamic looks. Then it dawned on me that even if I got the look right, using the concentric designs I saw on mosques and Islamic literature, what would be the message?

This confounded me. I learned quickly that I knew very little of counter-ideology, let alone creating posters. Plus, there was an expense to it, a cost in resources and time to do more research. Where would

I find information that the best minds in the world could not find to help defeat the ideas of extremism? I mean, every single researcher and social scientist out there had a reasoning on how to combat extremism. Yet nothing had worked so far. Most just called Muslims terrorists and Islam a terrorist religion, not openly but in other smart-language ways. Muslims saw through this and just walked away from all governments and researchers' efforts around that time. A few social scientists had great ideas, but they were complicated, like nation-building from the ground up in insurgency-ridden societies. Others talked of Islamophobia and racism, and some talked about how religious infrastructures needed moderation and overhauling as not to allow extremists space. These were great ideas, but you had to read a whole book of synopsis to figure this out. The majority kept highlighting case studies of the problems but offered solutions that sounded the same for everything.

Take, for example, the misuse of power and lack democratic space within Muslim communities globally. Their solution was to embrace democracy and democratic means in statements with nothing to back up how this could materialize. The issue of corruption destroying Muslim countries, their answer is end corruption not stating how it can be done other than we need for both cases civil society and means of accountability. I would read these researchers' documentation and marvel at how they understood the problem but really didn't bring any solutions. I grew up in Muslim community that had a hard-earned democracy thanks to the majority of Muslims and non-Muslims demanding it for a generation. Did these researchers not know that governments in the Muslim world maintain extremists to undercut secular democratic activism in their republics? That the so-called civil society is languishing in jails over simple things like tweets asking for democracy, let alone being allowed to organize, and we are the West deep in bed with them? The people are not stupid. They see it and shun our messaging because hypocrisy is built into our discourse. *How do I do things differently?* I thought. And then I thought what vanity or idiocy I must have had to even attempt doing so. I mean, I was barely one year college-educated, a proud blue-collar worker, and here were the smartest people on earth running in circles, along with our governments, trying to deal with this problem of extremism, up until that point in 2014. The governments did what they had to do: go to war, increase surveillance, and take all perceived threats out of circulation, which happened to be, well, the young Muslims succumbing to extremism across the world. Heck, dictators figured out that if they can label you a terrorist, they can Guantanamo you. Hence civil society and democratic activists for rights, liberty, and freedom got labeled terrorists along with real, active terrorists.

I didn't know how to make a poster, and more important, what was my message? I went back to research. I read and read Islamic scriptures, from the noble Quran, the holy book of Islam from Allah *subhanahu wa ta'ala*, to *hadith*, the sayings of the Prophet Muhamad, peace be upon him. I read them repeatedly, trying to understand that Islam is peace as I knew it and have seen it practiced all my life. I was looking for what I could find to support democracies and republics against the abomination that the majority believes is extremism of faith for terrorism. I did this while working as a manager for the retail store, being a father to my growing family and a caretaker of my parents. I was busy but happy. I was tiring my mind, body, and soul.

Here I was; I had the design of the poster figured out but did not have a message. I was reading and learning about my faith the noble Islam but did not understand it well enough to make any messaging from it. I mean, I understood it, but then again, I was no imam, clergy, or even a student of Islamic theology. One must be careful quoting scriptures if one fears being misquoted and misunderstood. I was, after all, a sinner but still a believer in an awesome God I called Allah *subhanahu wa ta'ala*. I hit upon the *hadith* that covered suicide. Islam, like all monotheistic religions including Judaism and Christianity, frowns upon suicide. Islam says those that commit suicide lose all hope of going to heaven. The faith of Islam, as in Judaism and Christianity, is predicated on the premise that there is a hereafter, an afterlife in which we are judged by our Lord to go to either heaven or hell. Believers of these faiths seek heaven as their destination.

What about suicide bombers, then? I mean, they put wires and bomb materials upon themselves or vehicles to detonate in the middle of people. All people. In mosques, markets, buildings, streets, churches, synagogues, temples, shrines, and just about anywhere that our government calls "soft targets." Not heavily protected zones. They kill women, children, and men indiscriminately. They never ask Muslims to move aside. The majority of those killed are fellow Muslims, even though we mostly hear about them when they kill Westerners.

What about the suicide bombers, then? I got my aha moment. So, it's true, they go to hell because they committed suicide. I went back to the Quran and found no mention there; maybe it is there, but I found it in the *hadith*, the sayings of our noble Prophet Mohammad, peace be upon him. I found three *hadith* from Sahih al-Bukhari's collections. Now, many *hadith* are contested, but Sahih al-Bukhari, who comes from Bukhara, in present-day Uzbekistan, is hailed as the preeminent scholar of *hadith* in the Muslim world.

If suicide bombers were called *mujahids* and *shahids*, those that died for the cause of Allah in jihad, the lesser struggle, were told they would go to heaven. But here was proof in plain sight, known to most Muslims across the world, that those that committed suicide go to hell. The *hadith* are explicit in how that is interpreted. For fear of doing the wrong thing, because I did not think it was that easy to debunk suicide bombings as an Islamic principle, I did what my father taught me when I had questions of faith. I sought out imams. I went to several imams in the Twin Cities. I asked, "Can these *hadith* be interpreted in the manner I was thinking, and is it in line with Islamic doctrine?" I met some of the most important individuals; out of concern for their anonymity, I will not mention their names, having not received permission to use them here. I approached four scholars of Islam: three men and one woman, from two schools of thought. They all said that the interpretation was accurate. I knew then that I had found something to use in the messages. This was a start.

Back to the posters, then. I found a student designer who could whip up the designs I wanted. I had the message ready: "What do you think happens to suicide bombers?" with the *hadith* below them. I mean, these were pieces of art. One poster had an X-ray photo of a suicide bomber with a vest showing the wires and a *hadith* below it. I had six different posters made and printed hundreds of each. Mind you, I was paying for this entire process myself. I was excited. I thought I would be the guy who revolutionized messaging against the concept of suicide bombing as an Islamic principle.

What a massive failure. The poster had too much on it; the words were a page long; the artwork was too complex, and even the people I wanted to target simply rejected it. I went to Muslim student unions at the universities and schools, and they said, "thanks but no thanks." I went to metro transportation authorities in the Twin Cities and across the country, asking them to put up the posters on buses in predominantly Muslim neighborhoods and cities. They took one look and rejected it. They said it did not meet their standards and they did not want to be associated with it. I went to mosques and got rejected outright. I tried to pay a local Muslim paper and an ethnic paper to carry the poster as advertisement; they rejected it too. I was demoralized by the entire process. After I lamented the outcomes to my family, they begged me, "Stop doing it and focus on living your life. You have a lot to be grateful for, to live for. You tried but failed."

Only my mother told me this: *"Waareya"*—which means *dude*— "I did not raise a quitter. If you believe in what you are doing, and it will help others, try and try and try again."

I am a mama's boy. I will not even hide that; this woman believed in me, always. Encouraged me, always. Pressured me to always do more, achieve more, get more, and to be pious in Islam. Up until that moment, I had failed in school and sold my business; I was a worker for a corporation after being a corporation of my own, raising four beautiful children, taking care of my father after he was paralyzed in a car accident, and trying my dammed best to create counter-ideology and failing at that too. Yet this Somali woman never gave up on me. My last supporter. I was tired and demoralized. I believed I had found the answer to a challenging problem. The world simply rejected it for low-quality, controversial topics and substandard messaging capability.

I am one who never gives up. Ever. A believer in words, especially the words of doers. Like Nelson Mandela, who said of dreamers, "A winner is a dreamer who never gives up." Giving up is never an option. "If I can think it, I can do it" was my philosophy in life. Plus, I was an American. Spell the word: Amer-*I-can*. This is not the land of quitters but of dreamers who go out to get a win. I am just an Average Mohamed, a proud blue-collar worker in America, but one thing I learned is that dreams are not cheap. Success is hard-won by tiring our minds, body, and souls. My mind, body, and soul were not tired. I still wanted to fight extremism using peaceful, nonviolent ways of messaging. Where there is a will, they say, there is a way.

Started on Video Productions. They Sucked. Cost Was Enormous.

What next? Failure, and not just failure but spectacular failure of process and concept idealization. Should I give up and say I tried and failed? I could not; something pushed me: my conscience. I watched as suicide bombers attacked American soldiers and the Muslim public across the world. I watched the news and got disgusted and said yes, I must be part of the solution. But how, then? I was watching Fox News showing a video of Jihadi John. Video—my second aha moment. That is what I needed to do to compete with ISIS, al-Qaeda, and al-Shabab videos. I mean, these videos were the reason our youth was being recruited. I knew this because in my research, I had read FBI transcripts of court cases brought by the heroes of justice, the Department of Justice, the attorneys general across America.

The most common message they said the tried and found guilty terrorists in court transcripts was first we were indoctrinated by clergy. Which clergy? One stood out: Anwar al-Awlaki, an American imam who I will go into details about later. Heck, I was just an average Mohamed, no better or knowledgeable in religion than Jihadi John. Even an Average Mohamed can stand up for the peace of Islam the same way Jihadi John stood for violence of extremism.

"What was it," the prosecutors asked, "that got you to join the death cults of al-Qaeda, ISIS, and Al-Shabab?"

They said it was that it gave them an identity. A *mujahid*, a revolutionary, an adventurer, a sex tourist with bridal promises bringing about a puritanical situation, hatred of our foreign policy, a new world order—a Jason Bourne, action-packed identity, being an agent of mayhem and death. Some people seek these things, and they offered them without remorse, law, and order, or even justice. They ruled by the gun and the mob of violence. Yet kids get caught up in this process in Minnesota, across America, and now, globally. How were they recruiting? Videos. ISIS had a production unit that made Hollywood envious in terms of funds and resources. From beheading videos to action-packed videos that showed regular kids doing amazing things for their victory against democracies and republics; from Africa and the Middle East to Asia; the amount of money spent on creating these videos was impressive. Posters were out as a concept of counter-ideology. Video productions were in. I got my second try at this effort of counter-ideology.

What did I know about video productions? Nothing. I was a businessman, not a videographer. But I knew of some videographers and artists in the field. My circle of people is wide because of my work as a retailer in the community. I've met hundreds of people a day in conversations, from getting coffee to getting gas, for over a decade. I talk to just about anybody to make that extra buck. But I love to talk and learn about people. I learn where they're at and what's good with them. People like that and engage you. This is the true art of conversation. My father taught me to be a conversationalist who would talk to the homeless and national leaders in the same way, with respect and dignity, recognizing their humanity and where they're at. He told me to talk first and learn a person; then you can take their money every day, not just today. I am the son of my father; he taught me, this man who was a third-grade dropout and a lover of languages who spoke eight: Somali, English, Arabic, Italian, Oromo, Amhara, Elay, Swahili, and Italian.

Who traveled the world three times over for trade and commerce. Buy something, sell something, from grocery stores to coffee, livestock, and commodities, including at a shrimp farm as the foot soldier for enterprises with his brothers and cousins. They called us the *Anfarta*, for we intermarried for five generations and our families are thick as blood. Family has always been the second side of my square life as a Somali man. Remember I am a square with four sides. The first being God. *If I save a life with this work, would I not be saving humanity as the Quran teaches?* I thought as I kept on reading the Quran, my lifelong passion as a sinner with the hope that one day, we shall live up to it and the standards of Allah. I was not evil like these folks who kill indiscriminately, not a saint as you would believe I was. Just an Average Mohamed. A regular *waareya* with his own issues. But this work I could do, I believed.

I called my friend, who wishes to be anonymous. I created a beautiful script that I believed, with his production abilities, would be a smash. The script was about playing chess. I marshaled my friends to volunteer to act—folks like me. One of them had just joined the navy. We created a scenario in which we asked why, if life were a game of chess, you would take yourself out in suicide missions. In essence, it was like the king capitulating in the middle of a game. That is what suicide bombers are, pawns in a game they can never win, sacrificed to make others king. Who are these others? The Osama bin Ladens and Abu Bakr al-Baghdadis. But even if they are taken out, more come into power as so-called emirs or leaders who seek power by sacrificing our youth with false promises that they will go to heaven, that they are *mujahids* and will die as *shahids* who will live forever. These false narratives and promises I was determined to create counter-ideology against, to create a counternarrative for. We went to production and made three scripts and videos. I spent thousands again. I was excited that now I had the formulation. I mean, if videos work for extremists, then videos will work for me too. Here I was, setting up in my house or the park or the gym to produce the videos. We made the videos and, excited, I went out and started showcasing them. But I had learned my lesson. In my research, I had come across the concept of market-testing a product.

I didn't want a repeat of the same process as the posters. What came next demoralized me even further.

I bought a small television set, put the videos on a CD-ROM, and made hundreds of them in production. I went to parks where Muslim youths would play basketball and soccer, to mosques, and even to civic arenas to showcase this product to the community. I was sure that this time I had hit the nail on the head. I had prewritten surveys to gauge responses. What came next shocked me. The folks unanimously rejected my message. I mean, the comments coming in the surveys were brutally honest. One of them said, "This is so cheesy; don't bring this nonsense to us." Another said, "The production is subpar, and the message is way off; you don't get us, the youths." Another said, "Stop this work; this is bad for us all. Please do not put it out there. I say this out of respect to you, for I know you to be a good person trying to do good." It went on like this for hundreds of surveys. Less than 10 percent thought it was a worthwhile effort. Ninety percent rejected it. Here I was thinking I had found the answer and the public was telling me it was the wrong way, the wrong answer. I was out thousands of dollars, time, and effort, and now my reputation was taking a hit along with my works. I was demoralized all over again.

How hard is it to create a message that the people can accept? I had spent too much money; my wife, who knew how much, was upset about it. You know a happy wife makes a happy family. I almost gave up. But giving up is not in my understanding. The war in Iraq and Afghanistan was heading the wrong ways. Attacks were happening across the world, from Mumbai, India to Catalan Spain; from Mogadishu, Somalia to Nairobi, Kenya; from London, England to Paris, France. The problem was becoming a bigger issue, and governments were literally yelling, "Do something, Muslims!" The media was calling us out. Where were the moderate Muslims who could counter this issue? It was a global challenge, and here I was creating duds and failures to respond as an Average Mohamed. The videos produced by ISIS alone were worthy of Hollywood-style productions, and mine were considered cheesy. "Get that away from us" was the common response by Muslim youths across the Twin Cities. It didn't work. We believe in ourselves, but reality has a way of kicking our butts and reminding us we are not all that.

As noble as my cause was, I was still producing subpar products for the market. This I understood clearly as a capitalist businessman. If you don't have the right product for the right market, you are throwing good money and efforts down the drain into waste. I was demoralized again. But failure is not acceptable in my mind. I never give up on my ideals, ever. That much I knew: the world deserved an answer to violence that is based on peaceful means and nonviolence, with messaging able to compete for ideas and minds. I understood clearly then that the hearts belong to another; for Muslims, it is Allah *subhanahu watta'ala*, for Christians Christ, for Jews Adonai, for Hindus Krishna or Ram or any deity they choose. And so on and so forth. Why was I failing in this process? Were my goals not noble? Was the market wrong?

It never is. This market is one of minds, to win minds for the causes of democracies and republics. For freedom, liberty, and rights for all against extremism. I took a break, took time out to reevaluate my understanding. I was out of money after paying for this process out of my own pocket. I was out of patience with those who loved me seeing me waste my potential pursuing a mission that so many, including governments, were having a hard time coming to grips with. My family, who I had little time to spend with, was aching for my presence. My kids had reached an age where they demanded more presence. My wife was upset because she could not understand why I needed to save others when we had real-life needs at home. My mother was upset that I didn't finish my education while cleaning toilets and serving coffee. Pressure came from all sides, and here I was, floundering and failing in all my efforts. I seriously thought about giving up, but something told me to go back and reevaluate again.

Came across Cartoons. "Eureka" or Epiphany Moment—the Kids Took to It.

I was missing something obvious, going about it the wrong way. I read my surveys again, this time not ignoring the negative ones but digging deep into them. One kid had said, "You know, we like cartoons. Instead of badly produced videos, use cartoons. We will watch even bad ones with a message."

That kid told me something I did not know. Again, I learned one thing in this process. I learned a valuable lesson. Education will save you money, time, and effort. Why did I not think of asking the kids what they preferred to see and hear? Why did I not investigate popular-culture engines? This was generation *Simpsons, Family Guy, South Park*, Nickelodeon, and Disney. They grew up watching cartoons from a young age and still do in their teens and early twenties. Well, had I spent my money getting an education at a university, I could have learned all this. But I am one who says, "Let me try it first and fail, learn, and try again and again and again." I am a dreamer who never gives up. When it comes to doing good for God, country, family, and a living, I go all out as a square in a world of radical change, from how we take off our shoes at the airport to the permanent surveillance of we Muslims across the world, denaturing our democracies and republics and orienting them toward safety over civil rights, liberties, and freedoms. I knew I had to do something, but what I was doing was failing spectacularly. *Should I give up?* I thought to myself one day in the doldrums of my failures. Maybe this kid understood something I was not getting.

Now, I love cartoons. I grew up on Mickey Mouse and Tom and Jerry, the Coyote chasing the Road Runner, and many more characters, from Tin Tin to Marvel and DC comics characters. I grew up going to the British Library in Mombasa to get cartoons in an age when we had only one television channel and Saturday was a cartoon-filled morning. I understood this kid's insight immediately.

Again, what did I know about producing cartoons? Nothing, absolutely nothing. I was a connoisseur of cartoons but never a producer of them. How would I go about producing cartoons? I started to research the process to develop what I wanted. At this juncture, you will understand that research and development is the key to any progress in anything. You can have an idea, and it could be marvelous or even revolutionary. But if you don't put the work in for research and development, then you are wasting your time. If you don't put your money and sweat behind it, you are just daydreaming. Dreams are precious commodities, which, as the world will remind you again and again, come with enormous costs. Failure is an important part of them. If you are afraid of failure, then get out of the heat of the process. Do not dream; do not attempt anything; be happy in the box of your reality. Be comfortable in whatever you are because you are afraid to fail. Failure is a learning tool in life. To be wrong is OK. To fail is OK. To give up when there is good work to be done is not OK. My mom, who is illiterate and never went to school, taught me this. She understood that in life challenges come and only those brave enough to face them will overcome. My educators and mentors through life told me not to assume. Assuming is wrong. Go out and do the work. Whether it is washing toilets and serving good coffee or trying to sell ideas, it requires three things: determination, perseverance in hard, consistent work, and resources. If you lack any one of them, then you will fail. You will fail and fall and not get up. Learn from your failures to improve and come harder at the issue to get a solution for success. When knocked down, do you not get up? Not getting up is like failing all those who came before you, that bloodline that came into you came through millennia of reproduction. You are no different than anyone out here, not dumber or smarter. What you lack another has in abundance, and what they lack you have in abundance. Finding the right fit to one another is a strategy-based, research-based effort. There are no shortcuts in life. Believe me on this one.

In this process of counter-ideology, I found rejection to be my common theme. I rolled up my sleeves and went back to work, working sixty-five hours a week at being a manager with eleven employees and generating over a million in income while raising a family, blessed to live in peace in a country where heroes, from police to federal agencies, maintain harmony, and taking care, as is my duty as a son, of my parents, who were now old and in retirement. This country we live in, America, asked very little of me and gave me the opportunity to do all this. I was determined to give back in my own way.

For this democracy and republic is a hand-me-down society, with values handed down from stranger to stranger, called citizens. I was a citizen by 2014. I believed I had the way to help my country and live up to the ideals of the third side of my square lifestyle, "for country." I am not a fanatical flag-waving kind of guy. I believe in America because Americans believed in me, welcomed me, and gave me opportunity in the corporate world, in our beloved Minneapolis and Minnesota. They provided for my parents' free health care and even paid them in social security benefits. My family came as immigrants. Yet in time my brother became a legislator in the Minnesota House of Representatives, my sister a professor with a PhD, my other brother a mechanic for planes, my other sister a businesswoman with an adult day care, my other sister an office manager for a health care company, my two brothers' truckers in America. We went from coming with only a bag, a T-shirt, and jeans to achieving the American dream. Here I was, a proud blue-collar American. I was determined to put in what we took out and will continue to take out for the good. I reached out to freelancers and did what corporate America did to us all: I outsourced the process of making cartoons. I reached out to India and talked to a Hindu guy who was an artist extraordinaire. I explained my vision to him. He explained how he could make it a reality. The process was broken down for me. First, write a script. Then create a voiceover for the script. Third, create videography for the script, a sequence of scenarios you expect to come about. Send it to him, then he creates it. Simple but complex. I needed actors for the voiceover. Gladly I was happy to try effort after much research into process of voice acting. I come from a large family, so I recruited my nephews, nieces, cousins, brothers, and sister into the effort along with using my voice. Why? Because I had less money to spend and they were free, the cheapest of all labor. You see, in my family of Somalis, we stick to each other thicker than blood. We help each other when it comes to communal ways. We support each other.

The same way I support them, they support me. This is the second side of my life being a square.

The question now was how to produce the voiceover. I found a white guy, a Christian, on 38th and Chicago, right across from my store, with a studio. When he saw what I was doing, he charged me nominal rates to produce the voiceovers. Here we were, Muslims, Christians, and Hindus, making a message, creating a cartoon about how to win minds, not hearts, because hearts belong to God, for the cause of liberty, freedom, and rights for all peoples. In essence, for America, which is diversity at work, black, brown, and white coming together and working for the good of humanity. This is what democracy is. This is what we were trying to convey in our messaging against the extremism of violent jihadis who would see it as an abomination—freely mixing peoples and ideas not controlled by them and their nihilistic vision of mayhem and murder. They wanted to bring about an order that would make me, the Muslim, supreme over the Christian and the Hindu guys in this effort—to make them less than equals and deny them equal access to their rights and freedoms, including their own lives. Therefore, I knew that this time, I must succeed in the process to safeguard this world we live in from the abomination of extremism.

We made our first message. It was about the concept of al-Shabab checkpoints in Somalia when they banned bras. Yes, al-Shabab at one point banned bras; for whatever reason, these religious nuts found bras-sieres worn by women to be immoral. What is it about men and trying to control women, especially what they wear?

I made my first cartoon. Lord help me, this one was not funny, and it bombed, but kids watched it anyway. The message was six minutes long, in English. It looked amateurish, and even the script sounded corny. But the message sunk in. The animation was excellent, and so were the voiceovers done by the white Christian guy. I don't use names, for anonymity, to protect my people. I will explain why later. I took the cartoon around and met some of the kids from before, and they were like, "You are improving, but this is too preachy. We don't have time to watch six minutes of boring educational stuff. Make it half that time at most."

I had hit upon a format the kids could watch from age eight to twenty-five in America. If it worked in America, then it could work in the world, I thought. I was so happy and reinvigorated. My "eureka" moment had come. The medium of choice was cartoons, not video or posters, to deliver a message.

The beauty of cartoons was their versatility. You could create scenarios of wanton destruction without destroying anything. No production setup, no actors, just animations. As in a dream, you could move from one concept to another seamlessly in a span of three minutes or less. It did not cost as much as video production but was more expensive than posters. Here I was paying for this process out of my pocket, using the money from the sale of the store. I had made a deal with my wife. I bought her a bigger house and a new car in exchange for letting me continue with my works. I spent time, energy, and effort, cashed in favors, begged, borrowed and—God forgive me—stole from my future savings to create this process. Again, my incentive was noble but human. I wanted to win minds in counter-ideology. I had just hit upon my epiphany about just how to go about doing it successfully with the best results that could be expected. I did what I do best as proud blue-collar man. I went to work writing scripts and creating cartoons. The question that came up was how I would then disseminate them. I mean, I could reach hundreds in parks, mosques, and madrassa, which means Islamic schools and other locations. But there was another place, the one my cousin had asked me about. What is social media? Because that is what drove the recruitment of my niece into extremism.

Understood Very Little of social media?

Next came the idea of using social media. Now, I knew what social media was. I mean, we were generation Myspace. Yeah, I am that old. We once had America Online for the internet and waited hours to upload a picture. I was familiar with Facebook from college, but this was a passing phase, I believed. I did what I always do: registered social media accounts as Average Mohamed. I started with YouTube and Google, then Facebook, and later Twitter and Instagram. I understood that simple-to-understand messages speaking to the common man's values and understanding would be my format, using Islam, logic, democracy, and freedom as the basis of my messaging ability. But I would use just about any logical means, from the Bible to the Quran, to make a message if the value was consistent with anti-extremism.

I knew this was where I could reach millions, so I got on social media as an Average Mohamed. The struggle began anew all over again.

Chapter 3
Now That I Have the Product Defined, What to Do With It?

The next frontier was social media. I knew nothing of it but the basics. You upload a video or post a comment and then you wait for your audience. There are platforms that are free. One thing you just have to love about America is that for every need, there is a commercial group of capitalists who will provide a service or product for your needs. YouTube is owned by Google, Facebook is owned by Meta, and Twitter is owned by a corporation. There are many who say these platforms are used to disseminate hate and extremism. Many a researcher has stated that. But I am one who they let spread hope and counter-ideology on their platforms. Governments in Europe and even here in America clamor to control them. Dictators, communists, and theocrats outright shut them down. Nothing has revolutionized the art of free speech and open communications in this world more than the free internet, especially social media. Therefore, the powerful fear it, and we, the nobodies, the average folks, rely on it. *Why not do the same thing the extremists are doing?* I thought.

According to FBI transcripts, some individuals were lured into extremism by social media postings. The teachings, videos, and sermonizing on social media accounts were intriguing to them. I saw the ISIS playbook for recruitment into extremism. It had a specific play for every scenario or outlook in life. If a young man needed identity, they gave him one; if young girl needed a husband, they arranged one. If the devout were seeking a more religious outlook, a society in religious harmony with the ways of the puritanical ones, they told them, "Come to us and you will find it." All of this was done from thousands of miles away, sometimes locally done with face-to-face recruitment. But social media played a role in it. My solution was that social media could be the conduit to express opinions and statements using popular culture tools like cartoons to deliver counter-ideology. Again, easier said than done.

If the video is about someone shaking their you-know-what and being provocative, you can rack up millions of views and likes. Is that the route I should go? Pay others to shake their you-know-what and be provocative? I did not like that—not that I don't enjoy those videos on social media. But how does one compete with beheading videos? With action-packed videos or videos made with humor, sensational and clearly designed to win minds of our youths, and effective at that process? I tried to watch those videos. My soul could not take it. My mind was repulsed by images of American soldiers being bombed and killed, civilians being bombed and maimed, and beheadings of whomever they could get their hands on that happened to be a Westerner or an Asian or African, anyone who was different from them and whom they called the enemy. From brave journalists and aid workers to just Christians, Hindus, Sikhs, Jews, and especially Muslims. *How can a mind accept this?* I thought. But what audacity to think I, just an Average Mohamed, could impact that process. I had hope and determination.

Put It on social media

Then I did what the violent jihadists did and put up my video on social media. Now, I am not religious but do believe in an awesome God. I prayed it would find the right audience. I put up the videos on YouTube and Facebook. I tell people God is good all the time. My prayers got answered as I lived and breathed. The videos went viral.

Many will say it is just lucky that you went viral. Luck has nothing to do with it. The messages came in an age when governments were coming after Muslims globally, with the media calling Islam a horrible religion in every segment of their news reporting. I mean, by 2014 or 2015, this was what Muslims felt and sensed and saw. To hear an Average Mohamed—not the clergy, not the government, not the media—saying "peace up, extremism out" was exactly what the world needed. The whole world responded. Tell me of a country and I will share your analytics of the message being heard, received, and promoted by Muslims, for Muslims. I was still paying for this process myself, learning as I was going along. I had no clue and am still learning today how to utilize social media accounts. I knew if I kept it simple and straightforward, common people like me—nobodies who don't speak in forked tongues like some in our governments and media—would appreciate our messages. My hunch was right. My mantra was and still is, "It takes an idea to defeat an idea." I went after the values of extremism I had learned about by researching why folks became extremists. I started the counter-ideology process using popular-culture-engine tools.

Learn What Algorithms Are. YouTube Sensations and Facebook Went Viral.

Social media is a valuable tool for an Average Mohamed. It equalizes the playing field, and as a capitalist, I immediately understood its value in reaching the masses at a cheap rate. "Cheap" was important because I was paying for this process myself from beginning to end. The way social media works is based on your habits. If you look at a certain message and like it, more messages along the same format will be sent to you. What this does is create a silo of messages that conform to your bias, be it news or information.

This process is generated by algorithms. These algorithms play a great role in what you see. At first, I had free rein on social media. I just put up the videos and they went viral. YouTube, Facebook, and others helped, through their algorithms, to spread the process. This is one reason why I am a big supporter of social media companies. I believe our governments want to limit them to stop free speech and open discourse that they don't control. A system of open processes scares governments, hence their directives to try to censor folks, coercing social media companies with do-it-or-else methods. Free speech is one thing we, the Average Folks, will not compromise about with the powerful. Even if you agree with the current crop of government on censorship of free speech, who says the next crop of regime of government you disagree with will not try to limit your speech. This is why I wholeheartedly support social media companies doing business unmolested. Leave our YouTube, Facebook, Twitter, and Instagram alone, because we, the citizens, will know how to use them eventually for the cause of freedom, justice, liberty, and rights around the world. Unless we want to join in with dictators, communists, and theocrats in censorship. Then what good is our democracy?

I learned how to use algorithms, how to put tags on messages, and started going viral again and again, whether the message was about identity; women's rights; suicide bombing as an un-Islamic principle; the promotion of voting over bullets, knives, and bombs; democracy; or just the plain old reteaching of Islamic values of peace. Average Mohamed videos kept on going viral around the world. Because they were all in English, and I made my products for America, for my country, I was surprised to see them get a global audience. I learned and studied analytics. YouTube has them; so does Facebook. They give you insights into how long a message was seen and watched, and by whom in terms of age, sex, and region. I was really surprised at how many commented on the videos and the number of likes in the height of 2014 to 2016.

I was still working sixty-five hours a week as a gas station manager to make commission and sales. I was still a father to my kids and taking care of my invalid father. In essence, I was living my dream. My American dream. The Average Mohamed dreams.

My dream is to live life as a square. There are four sides to my square. The first side is as a Muslim with a belief in an awesome God. I call my God Allah *subhanahu wa ta'ala*. I may be a sinner and not even a perfect Muslim, but I submit to the will of Allah. That does not mean I am religious, because I am very secular in my ways. It's a contradiction, but I believe God is good all the time. That God sees in our hearts our spirit and love and is mercy and grace to us, humanity. God is love. To fear God and his ways as best as we can is what I pursue, although I fail at it in the process. A struggle, or jihad, between my *nafs* soul and self. Sometimes the *nafs* wins and sometimes I win. But there are basic things I will never do, some things I can't help doing, and many things I try to avoid doing. This jihad is one in which I was failing but never gave up hope of redemption and revival, thanks to a family of conservatives and friends who kept on urging me to believe and pray constantly. Especially my parents, who I spent a lot of time taking care of. Islam is the greatest inheritance I got from them. I raised my kids in the madrassa and mosques in America beyond their education in school. Every child of mine will know the *hadith* and memorize the Quran, just as I was raised, by age fifteen. "Secular" does not mean abandonment of God. It means to accept that there are many ways to God. I am a Sufi of the liberal side of Islam. The live-and-let-live Islam. The "leave us alone, and we don't want to infringe on your faith" faith of my ancestors. My grandma and uncle indoctrinated me into Sufism, the meditations, chants, and *dhikr* way of life in addition to the prayers and incessant almsgiving. Giving does not mean just money in charity. A smile is charity; putting joy in others when talking is charity; laughing with humanity is charity; love for one another is charity. Treating other human beings, the way you want to be treated, with respect, dignity, and honor— these are the ways of Allah or God and his prophets. This is the first side of my square.

The second side is my parents, siblings, and extended family. To these I owe responsibilities that are binding by blood. They are my anchors in life. They never give up on me, and I will never give up on them. They are my backbone, my back-up, and then some. I am a child of the Somali people, born of the Darood tribe of the Majeerteen, born of the Issa Mahmud clan and subtribe is Abubakar Osman. I come from a family that has played a tribal role for hundreds of years, so that mantle of being responsible to the tribe and the tribal obligations of my people sits squarely on my shoulders too. As was my grandfather, uncle, and now, for the next generation, us we serve our tribe in leadership capacity. We aspire to fulfill our duty to our family of kin and folks. That includes all Somalis, for we are all close kin to one another before the rest of humanity.

The third part of the square is country. My country is America until I am told otherwise. To America I came as a youth; I have lived in America for longer than anywhere else on this planet. In this country I found myself with freedom, liberty, rights, and available opportunities at first. In this country I learned of a brotherhood and sisterhood based on an idea. The idea of America is *freedom*. That we were all created equal across race, gender, color, sexuality, religion, political affiliation, and any other creed. That we are all endowed with inalienable rights, and not even our government can take these rights without accountability. That pursuing justice and liberty is the pursuit of our happiness as a people. I found neighbors, friends, coworkers, and even some government folks with love in their hearts and acceptance in their extended hands. I found a cause I could believe in, a country worth accepting, for we are the freest people on earth. Why do I always say, "You just got to love America," folks asked me. Well, my family and I came as immigrants to this country. My brother is a legislator in the Minnesota house, my sister a professor at a university, my other brother a technician for planes, my other brothers truck drivers, my sisters in the healthcare industry, and another with her own business. Can you imagine that we came with nothing but a bag of clothes and the jeans, T-shirts, and hijabs we were wearing to get our American dream within our lifetimes? For our kids to get a free education? American taxpayers paid for our education and for my ailing parents and paralyzed father, who got free health care due to their age. I lived in peace thanks to our heroes who diligently work for peace: our police, soldiers, spies, and diplomats. We enjoyed prosperity and upward mobility as we moved from being immigrants to citizens of the greatest country, which allows this transformation to happen in less than a generation. America deserves undying, unwavering, unstoppable loyalty and honor from me. This is a great country. I'm not saying there are no imperfections or problems living here as a Black man, a Muslim activist, foreign-born and a Republican too. But the good in America—its people, with open hearts and open hands extended in friendship, who I have lived with and made a home with—this, by far, surpasses all the bad. Just like everything else in life, the yin and yang of it, the good in America far outweighs the bad. In essence, our American dream, with hard work, ingenuity, sweat, imagination, and innovation, can be achieved here. My family is living proof of it.

The last side of the square is making a living. Make a living, for there is dignity in work, a dignity that is unsurpassed in offering value to you. Therefore, I pride myself on being the best toilet washer in America even as a midlevel manager who can delegate the toilet-washing to others. If someone pays you a dollar, I say give them a dollar fifty's worth of work to keep them coming, and next time they might offer you two dollars. I am an avowed capitalist. Not a pig, for it is not halal, but one with a soul. I do not dream of being filthy rich; that has never been my dream. If it were, I would not be spending my own money, hundreds of thousands, on self-funding counter-ideology means. But I do so self-fund this process to help me be in good standing with God, country, and humanity. Otherwise, I would have spent that money on starting a new business venture and securing riches from doing business comes as second nature to me. To make a buck, one way or another, is easy for me out here in the world. For I don't mind manual labor and can work easily as a blue-collar worker or manager in any organization, from running a business to working with communications. We learn in this global world that one must hustle. Make your hustle more than one. Currently, as I write this book, I'm working on four ventures. I work part-time as a manager at a clothing store, run a nonprofit, and opened a food manufacture company making Mossa Samosa, which I will explain later. And I opened a political action committee called Republican People of Color, an advocacy group.

This makes me a square, which I pride myself in. Many think that to change the world one must expose themself to extremes or be a radical. Average Mohamed espouses moderation and anti-extremism. I have no political ambition to run for a seat, although I have been asked many times to do so by Republicans and community members. But just like everyone, I am a partisan. My politics are simple. Espouse freedom, liberty, rights, opportunity, and justice for all. Support conservative movements. Promote peace against hate be it religious, racial, or ideological in nature. Live with responsibility toward family and country, with all my opportunities and equal rights. In essence, it's not good enough for me to live free; I must seek freedom for all humanity too. No exceptions, no exclusions. Whether your politics are of the right, like mine, or the left, like those of my brother, the Democratic legislator in Minnesota, it is we squares who change things and create a better world. I don't use names because I want to give anonymity to my family too. I will explain why later. I was and am still living the square lifestyle in activism, business, political, and family life, a simple code to me living as an Average Mohamed. The simpler it is, the easier to try to live up to it. I am honest to say success is hard to come by, and I'm failing in all spheres of being a square but determined to get it right one day. Maybe you are better off than me in your code in life.

Chapter 9
Global Minnesota and Schools Reach Out

Media Attention. Local Paper *Star Tribune* Got Me Rolling.

Media attention picked up on the viral videos. The *Star Tribune,* a local Minnesota newspaper, got me rolling. A reporter called and interviewed me. I was hesitant at first. Media is not the best of friends to people of color, Muslims, foreign-born Americans, and even Republican-leaning activists. But my mission was to get as many audiences and eyes to see my message as an Average Mohamed could. Here the media could play a positive role. But I had never done an interview before. What were the procedures and means of communicating via media? Like everything else, I had to learn. The article came out, and as everything else had, it went viral too. Then more medias came calling and asking for interviews.

The questions were the same throughout. Who are you? Why are you doing this? What are your goals? Who is paying for this process? How can you prove your method works?

From the Public Broadcasting Service, *The New York Times, The Washington Post,* and Breitbart News Network, from papers to the left and the right, they came, and I interviewed with them. Then came the international papers: *The Guardian, Financial Times, The Times of Israel,* and many more. I found success in media because I repeatedly studied my statements and comments. I read and reread them to see what I said and what was printed in the papers. Then I observed my body language and speech mannerisms on television interviews.

Then came radio; oh, I love radio. I love public radio the most and even fund it as a donor. On radio I just relax and speak from the heart without worrying about facial expressions. I find radio to be the most effective way, along with podcasts, for me, Average Mohamed, to deliver a message. I can be true without the vanity of how I look, but the sound of my genuine voice comes across. I hail from a people who are constant in speech and telling messages. Coming from a background as a lover of poetry, I speak in poetry to explain reality.

Learning How to Talk to Media: Observing Talk Shows on Cable to Learn How to Talk.

I learned how to speak to the media. My research was based on the media itself. I watched and read so many articles and news show and listened to radio shows. I dissected what was said and how it was said. Was it effective to reach me, the average guy? What did people around me think of it when I shared it?

Here is what I learned: I would, in the beginning, pontificate for minutes at a time to answer media questions, giving complex answers to a complex problem. I would do an hour-long interview only to see thirty seconds of it used. This frustrated me. Then I came across the understanding that print space, airtime, and pictures were limited. There are so many causes out here in the world competing for eyeballs and ears to try to change the world for better. All are good causes that deserve attention and your mind space. What made mine, the Average Mohamed's, any different from theirs? What made my works as important for you to look at and listen to, watch, or read? Passion is one thing, but every human being is passionate about one thing or another. What gave me the right to intrude on your mind space unless you were going to gain from it? I could speak for ten minutes at a time until the reporter, tired, overworked, and in a hurry to meet a deadline, cut me off. Passion alone is not good enough, I learned in mass communication to the masses. I watched CNN and FOX News daily. I watched the evening news, all of it, daily. I read so many papers and listened to Minneapolis Public Radio and Republican-leaning outlets, including Rush Limbaugh and Sean Hannity, daily. I learned how they communicate with people. I did not discriminate, and I don't today, from left to right. The way of communicating truth exists on both sides, but left to your own decision, what is your truth?

I learned that a news segment is usually no more than two minutes, and in-depth ones are three minutes at most. The reporter or interviewer takes up a minute and a half of the allotted time explaining the issue in detail, and you have fifteen to thirty seconds to make your pitch, to espouse your cause on television. In print, they ask you a detailed question, and you spend no more than thirty seconds to a minute answering it. Why I love radio is that you are given more leeway. You have a little more than a minute, maybe up to a minute and a half, to speak. Here you are passionate and gung-ho about your cause and works, believing, like Average Mohamed does, that they could save lives and society from extremism, hate, and in defense of democracy—in essence, in service of freedom. So do all the other causes believe they are doing good on behalf of humanity. God is not for all, for some do not believe, and that is OK by us; as humans it is their choice. Country is not held in loyal esteem by all; some dissent out of their reality-based understanding. And that is OK because dissent is patriotic in America. Here I was, doing my works for God, country, and humanity, knowing this is the true passion I have. To serve God even though I was a known sinner, to help my country, securing gains for it and humanity, for what is good for America is good for humanity, I believed. What some in the world do not believe in our God or our country, given the plurality of understanding of things. And that is OK in America. I may be a believer, but that does not translate universally. How then was I to reach the masses, not just Muslims but non-Muslims, Americans, and non-Americans: the humanity in all of us?

I came to the epiphany that the most common denominator is speaking in sound bites. A sound bite is a short extract from a recorded interview chosen for its pungency or appropriateness. Words like "Peace Up, Extremism Out." "It takes an idea to defeat an idea." "You just got to love America." Harsh words like "bigots" and "haters," realistic words like "it sucks" . Simple words anybody anywhere could understand and relate to. It worked like a charm, all this effort learning to do interviews. I got called to be on over eighteen hundred interviews globally, from Timbuktu to Tajikistan, Israel to Bahrain, London to Washington, Nairobi to Mogadishu. I have been interviewed and spoken in sound bites from the mainstream media to the ethnic media. Muslim media loved this Average Mohamed the most. I was getting mail by the thousands with support from people of all kinds. Muslims were proud I stood up and spoke of the peace of Islam; non-Muslims were happy to learn about the peace of Islam. They had seen only the extremist version of Islam until then. They were happy for the opportunity to see a different understanding of most Muslims in the world.

Global Audience Found

I found a global audience. My videos went even more viral. I quickly learned to add one more skill set to my ways of communicating sound bites and messaging: cultural competency. I may be a secular and Westernized Muslim in my ways and thinking, but the community I wanted to reach was the majority, not Westernized or seeing themselves as secular. I was watching and reading what was happening in counter-ideology in Iraq and Afghanistan. Even I could see the coming failure. It was patronizing, moral superiority, and supremacy of ideas—nonsense, for lack of a better word. It could never relate to the Afghani or Iraqi, let alone Muslims globally. The violent jihadi propagandist figured out how to reach the Muslim masses with ideas and narratives faster than our multibillion-spending Western governments in counter-ideology. I mean, our governments spent our tax money in the hope of buying loyalty with ideas foreign to the Muslim people, speaking not to the values they did have but to the values they should have. What a colossal failure in imagination, cultural competency, or even basic understanding of cultures and religions in discussing ideas. In essence, we Western-ers went to create a Washington in Kabul or Baghdad, forgetting that Kabul and Baghdad had their own rhythms and ways that superseded Washington's, in cultures that were ancient and a religion older than any Western democracy.

I mean the pork; that is what we call the fat excess of the Western po-litical establishment, which bought into its own myopic view of the world and thought it knew better than existing cultures and society. The entire premise was predicated on outright disrespect of the closest-held values of Muslims. Media helped propagate the values because they wanted to show the people back home, "Look, we are better than these cultures, religions, and societies." They lacked the understanding that good exists in all cultures, religions, and worldview. I mean, it was a bonanza for suit-wearing experts who told governments what they wanted to hear and delivered an absolute disaster in Muslim and non-Muslim relations with their counter-ideology. Our government paid them and kept on paying them to continue with works that, when honestly evaluated by we Muslim activists, who were left to pay for our activism ourselves, would cause us to shake our heads. But the closed-minded community of government and lobbyists, matched with connected researchers to back up their nonsense, got us nothing in winning minds and hearts. I mean, every government agency was spending money on these folks, and Muslim activists like Average Mohamed were on the outside watching incredulously as they wasted away our collective tax money, backslap-ping each other for job well done while we were losing the minds and the hearts of Muslims, which we will never get, ever, globally. For the heart belongs to God. Do not take my word for it. Check out Gallup polls about the understanding of and support for America in Muslim countries over the last two decades. See if they like us or trust us as a country. Google it, please.

Let me start with a misnomer. The gall of using the adage "winning hearts and minds" as if folks around the globe are going to fall in love with us as Westerners is just plain stupid. Excuse my language, but this is my biggest frustration in this process of counter-ideology. We can win minds, for humans are rational once we culturally competently connect with them, not as a Westerner or an Easterner but as a human. We can rationalize our feelings about what every average person wants in this world: freedoms and to get shelter, health care, education, and opportunity for themselves or loved ones. This is universal in the world. You don't need to be a genius to figure this one out. What do the violent jihadists promise their theocracy will make? A better hereafter, because they know they cannot deliver on a better here-today society with their brutality, killings, murder, mayhem, and global order. What all extremists offer is a puritanical world of themselves and their violent discarding of others by first hate of other Jews, Muslims, Christians, LGBTQI+ people, Blacks, Browns, disabled people, women etc. Then comes violence. As Westerners, we can win minds by explaining a society, like we do at Average Mohamed, that accepts diversity and plurality of understanding, that includes conservative and not just liberal Western values, which are closest to Islam in thinking are all welcome. Instead, we wanted to create a Washington out of Muslim lands and peoples with the guts to say we will win their hearts too. Such dumbness is an epidemic in the West. How could they not understand the simplest of concepts that a Christian can tell them? Their heart belongs to their God, not to men or women, no matter how benevolent, which any Muslim can tell the entire West. You have a chance at winning our minds, but our hearts they belong to Allah *subhanahu wa ta'ala*. The same goes for every people. Their hearts belong to their nation, not ours; their cultures, not ours; their society, not ours; and their ways, not ours. Yet here were our presidents and secretaries of agencies, all the way to aid workers on the ground, spewing this nonsense. We are winning hearts and minds. The question an Average Mohamed asks all humanity is this one where is the hearts and minds we won? After spending trillions in Iraq and Afghanistan, we may have won some minds among those who economically gained from this process and built a kleptocratic system. That is who benefited the most. Those Iraqis and afghanis like us and connected Westerners or who said what we wanted to hear only. What do they call it? The spin. Only this spin was from our pockets to those in government to those allied with our government, usually ex-government officials, to local foreign kleptocrats and despots. The people could see all this and knew and understood the game of this process. People, average people, are not stupid. So then, how many hearts did we win if even the most brutal of forces can defeat us in winning minds, as happened in Afghanistan? This is the West; dumb ideas get shelved to be used again elsewhere in another fashion. They said the same thing in the Vietnam War too. Expect for our governments to say the same thing again soon, in another conflict, and pork it out.

I swore not to go that route. I would rather pay to do what I want to do for the good of humanity than compromise to local despots' values and our government's systems of reciprocity with only itself and not the people or humanity. But that meant asking my government to allow Muslim activists to do what we wanted to do, the real work of winning minds and never uttering "hearts," for they belong to Allah *subhanahu wa ta'ala*. Our Average Mohamed works to do it within our cultures, our religious understanding, and when not in religion then according to human rights, human dignity, relevance, and an understanding of the modern world. That does not mean we can't espouse democratic means. Even the tribes in Afghanistan and Iraq exercise, like all tribes, a form of democratic egalitarianism. They practice Islam. The arrogance and stupidity to want to turn them into us is nothing short of a cultural-slavery mentality on the part of Westerners. It is cultural slavery to say, "Yes, we are secular." That means abandoning our cultures and religions. I believe the assimilation of people into the global order of things should be based on the expansion of cultural understanding beyond just what we can accept or prefer. If they do them and the society is happy about it, let them do them. We do us. To each their own ways, but with a common understanding that we strive for freedoms as defined by the people, their people, for their people and of their people. Instead of trying to manipulate, we let them meet their destiny. Their destiny is theirs and never was ours. How, then, could we have been so arrogant as to claim we were not only winning minds but hearts too? Such hubris is what led to the downfall of civilizations. They failed to adapt to reality, as cold as a diamond and even harder but something even a child can understand. Money changes minds, and stupid ideas live on today. The next time you hear someone say we are winning minds, ask whose minds? Or are we culturally competing against their values, not assimilating them? If they say they are winning hearts, remember Afghanistan and Iraq. Afghanistan, we left to the Taliban and Iraq to the Iranian-backed militias. In essence, according to the understanding of Westerners with this ideology or idea, we lost minds and hearts to them. Nothing could be further from the truth. The people hate the Taliban and Iranian militias but can do nothing, since empowerment in our Western system meant abandoning theirs, which these misfits of humanity took advantage of and became defenders and promoters of what was theirs: culture, tribal ways, and even religion, be it sects or understandings. Yes, we won minds, but if we won hearts too, the Taliban and Iranian militias in Iraq would be facing firestorms today in their respective countries. Instead, it is we Westerners facing it, even after American taxpayers spent $6 trillion on the effort.

Average Mohamed will never claim to win hearts. That is dumb. What we will claim as our mantle is the promotion of freedoms in the hope that we can win minds by any means of nonviolence and the peaceful use of free speech and communication. By countering ideologies in the hope that an idea can defeat an idea. Promoting "peace up, extremist thinking out." Getting it in sound bites and slogans, using one methodology or another, from social media to mainstream media to independent media. The goal remains the same: we hope to win minds. Why win minds? For the cause of global freedom and people's power. Being willing to learn and improve means doing so constantly, achieving success elusive even to our multibillion-spending government in getting effective results that are quantifiable and researched.

Chapter 5

Students Told Teachers; Teachers Invited Us to Speak.

A teacher called me and asked if I was the Average Mohamed creator. I said yes. The next question she asked was if I would come speak to the students in her high school social science class. I was frank. I told her I was a gas station manager and an activist. I didn't know anything about teaching in a class. She said, "Come talk to me and I will guide you."

This teacher was from Roosevelt High School in Minneapolis. I went to see her, and she told me that her students told her about me. They asked I come speak to them. This was a revelation to me. Students were asking for me to come speak to them. I asked which students. She said they knew me from the gas station as a manager. *Huh*, I thought. Another issue came up that I was ill-prepared for. I was an old man talking to kids. This generation has its own reality that I can see, but that does not mean I can relate to it. I was scared at first. I told the teacher I would think about it. *Am I having an impact?* I thought. Because I did not think this process through in its entirety, I was content with social media means. That was my intention. This meant taking time off work during weekdays, and I needed the income to pay for the messages.

This also meant me going before kids in their environment. Now, if you know anything about me, you know I proceed only after I master the art of what I am trying to do. Again, I researched the process. Did you know American teachers get certified and are highly educated group of people? They are also very underpaid and work under conditions that would annoy any parent or citizen. The schools are always underfunded, and teachers' environments are very controlled, to the point that they just do their jobs under conditions that are not favorable. The more I researched, I learned that the kids had the best source of knowledge in their teachers, but the teachers did not control the kids the way I was controlled in Africa while getting an education. The American kid is an independent thinker and determines their own opinions about things. They are vocal and will speak their minds. I could not fathom talking back to a teacher back home, but that is an everyday thing for teachers here. I was getting paid to wash toilets and serve coffee and gasoline with better benefits than our teachers, just so you understand the value we put on our educators in America. Why would I go there and into their process for this work?

I debated the pros and cons of this process as I do with everything else in life. The pros were that I would get access to kids and could speak to the dangers of extremism and hate and the beauty of democracy, our collective systems and diversity and pluralism. You know who takes all our kids and teaches them that, plus more, in America? Our teachers. I came to respect teachers and what they face. This is an underpaid, understaffed, and unappreciated group of Americans doing the most important, crucial work of our democracy and republic, creating the productive citizens of America. Heck, I was just a gas station manager. What right did I have to come into their classrooms and take their place for this anti-extremism, pro-democracy cause I believed in? Who was I compared to them?

I told my mother of this process and explained to her my dilemma. This would mean a commitment. My mother never went to school but made sure all her kids got educated. She is being true to Somali mothers is cheerleader in chief of her children. The pressure of always asking me, "When are you going back to school get a degree and stop being a coffee server and toilet washer?" This time she was a cheerleader. She calmly talked about the prophets of Islam, which mostly we share with Judaism, and Christianity. She said each one of them came as a teacher to their people. "America is our people and our country now," she said. "We owe something to them, and if the teacher sees you like I do, as a person with high intelligence and means, why not go to the school?"

Only a Somali mother would bring up prophets talking about her children. I told her, "Mama, I am good at what I do because I don't do things halfway. I go all the way into the process once I make a commitment. *Hooyo*, I am no prophet. Just an Average Mohamed who is also a sinner, and lord knows she keeps on telling me to become a better Muslim and go get everything in this world. She was never happy with where I was but constantly urged me on nicely, the way mothers do. Go do more, get more, and achieve more—the cheerleading part.

She then told me, "You never know if you don't try whether this would be a fit for you or a waste of time and talents." I am a mama's boy. My biggest supporter in life is my mama, *hooyo*. This typical of Somali mothers. They just keep on pushing and pushing and pushing. Growing up, this was pressure, but now I had kids of my own, and I came to appreciate her undying persistence and urgings. I called the teacher back and spoke. I would do it, come to her class and speak to the kids, despite my misgivings about it all.

My Fears

I had fears. Part of me was afraid. I was last in a classroom in high school more than a decade before. I was older, not hip to this age's understanding. What if the kids responded negatively? What did I have to say to them? How would I say it to them? Did they have projectors in school to show the messages? Which messages do I focus on?

Then there were the basics. How should I look when presenting to them? I didn't have a suit; should I wear a *thobe* as a Muslim, like I do on Fridays, or even just my blue-collar attire of jeans and T-shirts? Or should I invest in Nike and Adidas to look hip in the presentations? I didn't know what to do. But I knew I made the commitment to go and speak to them. When I give my word on anything, I keep it. I went out and bought my second suit. The first one, I bought for my wedding. I bought a suit, shaved my face and hair, bought a tie, and even applied cologne. Vanity was creeping in, but I wanted the kids to see a secular, regular dude. Just their average neighbor with a cause.

My other fears were about my reception. What if the kids, some of whom were Muslims, think this topic to be a taboo that, like our government, media, and society, was blaming Muslims for the problem? What if they listened to my message and then said, "He is part of them too?" This topic of extremism needed certain aspects of sensitivity about it. It's a heavy, big problem that we Muslims just don't talk about because 99.99 percent of us are not extremists out to do harm to society. We're citizens just trying our best to live life free and go for our American dreams or humanity's dream. What was I getting into, and what would be the dividend of this process?

The cons: No resources for this process. I would now have to give more time and energy of myself again. The other one is more scrutiny by others. Nobody likes that; why expose myself further The last of the fears was, "What if I really suck at this process?" I was highly opinionated. Remember, I said teachers are highly educated people trained to keep their opinions to themselves—well, most do, anyway, but not all. Here I was, a known capitalist, a budding Republican, and an activist. How would they respond to that? The kids that live in a state heavily dominated by those who roll with the Democrats, the donkey side of things, and me being an elephant, a Republican. What was my message to a class of mixed religions, races, sexualities, nationalities, and political opinions—in essence, a mini-America? What would I say to win them all to our collective thinking? What format do I use to deliver the message? Orally, through works and homework, or through a presentation with a question-and-answer session? I listened to TED Talks and watched YouTube videos made by teachers to learn what they did that was effective in classrooms. They did a lot of work. My fear was of coming out flat and boring. I hated boring teachers. How would I make my presentation exciting to keep the kid's attention? I had more fears than knowledge of what I was about to do. I remembered my mother's advice, and it gave me courage, but I had butterflies in my stomach that antiacid relievers could not control. I wanted to be the best at this work. I researched and researched. I decided the best way to do this work was through a presentation of no more than fifteen minutes, followed by asking questions about lessons imparted for fifteen minutes and then taking questions for fifteen minutes. I was to deliver only three messages to the kids, create a lesson plan around them, and then do a survey of what the kids thought of my presentation.

When Kids See Honesty and Truth, They Relate. They Spot a Phony from a Mile Away.

I walked into the classroom, took half a bottle of Pepto Bismol medicine to calm my stomach, and made my presentation. The kids were quiet and listened. I asked questions that reinforced the values of anti-extremism, diversity, and plurality in America. Is it the strength of our democracy? The kids answered smartly. Then came their questions. I had two choices for how to answer them: toe the line and speak authoritatively or speak in truths. I was not a politician or government agent or even paid for the event. I chose to speak in truths. The Black, Brown, LGBTQI+, and Muslim kids asked if America was a bigoted country. I spoke the truth. As black people we came to America on ships, as slaves. Upon the end of slavery came Jim Crow laws, then the civil rights era, up to the time we had a Black man as president, President Barack Obama. This, by any standard, is a change in the right direction for our American republic and democracy. Is there structural racism? Yes, but can it limit you? *No*, because we Americans of all stripes, creeds, colors, religions, and races are fighting it every day, from our politicians to government agencies to civil society led by the corporations of America. We are not there yet, to a place where we black, brown, Muslim, or LGBTQI+ people can claim we are equals. But we have come a long way as Americans from our ancestors' conditions.

Then I challenged them: What can you do here in this classroom where all are equals sitting next to one another? I pointed to their diversity, in which a Tyrone, a Smith, an Abdi, a Jose, a Xiang, and a Sharon sat next to one another in an environment that the taxpayers of America paid for to keep the lights on and hire teachers to educate them. Black, Brown, Asian, White, Muslim, Jew, and even some with different sexualities.

"Do those things matter to you at all?" I asked them.

And they answered, "No, not with our generation, not most of us." I spoke the truth of the matter. They base their decisions on whether something is cool or not. It is not cool to be a bigot, to have hate in your heart, when love is easier. It is not cool to follow the enemies of our republic and democracy who want to tear down our diversity and plurality. Say no to extremism, hate, and anti-American sentiments.

The second most popular question I got was from Muslim kids. "What do we do in a society that see us as a threat?" I told them the truth: talk to your black and brown friends. They have been called threats all their lives and look how they deal with it: by being true to America. One in which they never gave up on America. That is exactly what those promoting the "enemy face" of Muslims want us to do: to give up in America our democracy, plurality, diversity, and laws for their hate, extremism, and anti-Americanism. I told them there is more love in America than the vitriol of hate espoused by some media, government officials, and politicians. Their role is to divide us to gain power, control, and budgets over us when they successfully define us as the enemy that needs to be controlled, monitored, and limited in means.

The perennial question I get from Muslims is about how we deal with the open-ended surveillance of our communities. I speak the truth again. Read the history of America to understand. The native nations were the first enemies of America, followed by black people, then Hispanics. But read what happened to Germans in America during the World Wars; their counterparts—Italians, Norwegians, Finns, Swedes, Serbians, and Japanese born in America—were considered enemy aliens. Read about how signs in America said, "No Irish or dogs allowed." Then learn what happened to Jews during the red Bolshevik scare in America. This is part of America too. We are the new group, and our teeth will get kicked in by some of them. Especially by our government if they have no fear of accountability. But if you are good and do good in life. You have nothing to fear. Even at the worst of times, these communities of Americans had allies who protected them from the Underground Railroad, abolitionists, and civil rights activists to political movements. Our democracy gives us tools to do so protect our rights, liberty, freedom and opportunity in America until that day when all can and will be equals. But do good and be good and you will have nothing to worry about, for your Constitution in America will serve you well.

The last most popular questions kids ask me is, "I don't like what is happening in the world; what can I do to help change it?" I tell them the truth. Those who can write, speak, organize, and reach out to humanity end up changing the world. Join politics because politics will want to change, you so change them. Join with other like-minded people, be they conservatives or liberals, but if you are passionate about what you believe, go act on it beyond posting "it sucks" on social media. Volunteer and act. But first get educated and know your stuff about the issue you want to change in the world.

What you don't do is join the radicals and extremists. They will fail in America and humanity because they are flamethrowers. Just like all fires, they combust and fizzle out. The way forward is moderation and activism in your causes at whatever level you feel content to play in this world. That they, the kids of America, live among the freest people in the world. The must use their freedoms. Many Americans gave it all for them to have those freedoms. Do not waste it or believe you cannot change an aspect of the world for the good of the world. Look at me, a nobody, and what I am doing. Who says you kids cannot do the same?

Learning Process. The Kids Taught Me Things.
More teachers across Minnesota started calling me. I accepted all invitations. I had a formula, a program, and a model. Presentation, my

questions, their questions, and speaking honestly with no spin. Kids are innocent; they can spot a phony message a mile away. Our kids are way smarter than we were at their age, thanks to access to information that we used to get from encyclopedias and history classes alone. They get it instantly on Wikipedia, Google, and social media. Do they the kids have biases? Yes, but can we talk honestly to them. The response I got back was a yes. I base that on Average Mohamed survey questions.

I asked if they had they seen extremist or hate messages on their social media and internet. Ten out of ten kids answered yes. Did the message of Average Mohamed have any relevance to their lives? Eight out of ten kids said yes. Does our program help understand extremism and hate? Seven out ten kids said yes, it did give them a better under-standing. Would they seek this information on their own? Only two out of ten kids said yes. After all, this was educational material, such boring stuff compared to what is out there for their eyes and minds. My competition is the latest dance craze or challenge. At that time, they were talking about pouring cold water over themselves as a challenge.

More schools across America started calling me to speak, then universities, mosques, madrassa, churches, synagogues, and civil society organizations. I spoke to tens of thousands in outreach across America; then came the world. I was working and making time thanks to my corporation, Speedway America—at that time Super America—which let me live this life if I kept on making them a good profit and it did not affect work. I was proudest when mosques, madrassa, churches, and synagogues asked for me to speak. The imams wanted to talk about extremism but were afraid or didn't know how to go about it without alienating their flock. I come into the room and present their teachings based on their collective values, and then they take over the process. This was the height of Muslim fears over extremism. In the Twin Cities, some parents were hiding their kids' passports because of fears that their kids had a risk of being brainwashed by joining in with extremists. The parents came and brought their kids to the functions. The churches and synagogues were curious. I mean, mostly, the liberal ones wanted to know how they could help Muslims in America stop the problems of extremism. As a matter of fact, in the beginning, it was mostly the liberals of America who had an open-door policy at this time for Muslim activists to speak at their events and venues. Then came the conservatives when they realized our message fit in with their values too. I spoke to Catholics, Jews, and Protestants alike. I spoke to Mormons and even atheists in America. They all welcomed me with open arms and open hearts. That's why this is the greatest country in the world, as I keep repeating. Not because I got an open-door policy but those others, despite differences, opened their minds to what we had to say as Muslim activists. I mean, they let an Average Mohamed come speak to them. I always spoke in truths. When I didn't know or have an answer, I told them the truth. Hey, I am not an important know-it-all person. Just an Average Mohamed, with a high school education at that time, who had opinions and a message of hope: that with our ideas we could counter, , promoting freedoms for all humanity.

I learned a lot from these public speaking engagements. I learned our kids are smarter and know more than we think they know. They have passion and, with a little hope and guidance, can do almost anything in activism. They are vocal and will tell you what they think eloquently. More eloquently than I could at most times. I learned the peer methodology of letting kids speak their minds in an open, safe environment where regular citizens conversate. Independent of positive reinforced minders and authority, they the kids themselves would pull the kids who were on the borderline of extremism or thinking extremism was cool. Teachers, mentors, and educators would call me, politely point to a group of kids, and say, "Please focus on them." Teachers know things that parents don't pick up on. After all, we send our kids to spend more time with them than we spend with them. I was always conscientious about focusing on those kids and asking what was good with them, what they thought of things, and what they needed help in. I never corresponded with them in writing because extremism is a national security issue. I did not want them to be flagged because I reached out to them and spoke in depth with them. There is no protection for Muslim activists, and I was designated as one by the state. On this matter, any anti-extremist activist can be labeled an extremist for their works. Trusting the system is not my strongest point. Distrust of government does not mean hatred of government. It just means we take extreme care not to harm others or create harm by our works. Surveillance is to Muslims in America what apple pie is to American culture. It is what it is. After all, the enemy they seek wears no uniform and has no profile. People need to be sorted out. The last thing I wanted was to be the reason a kid got placed under surveillance. I would turn off my phone and speak citizen-to-citizen. The kids would tell me politely, just speak to so-and-so; he watches those extremist videos and likes them. I would get that kid to come along and speak to the other, explaining what would happen to him or her because of extremism. I am to deliver a message of redemption and hope, nothing more. Anything beyond that I was not equipped to deal with, and our government, up until that point, was not offering Muslim activists the resources or means to develop like Europe, Asia, and the Middle East were doing in their societies. In fact, we were held at arm's length, except those hand-picked by our government, who were mostly only Democrats at this time because they rolled with Democrats, not because they were effective Muslims activists having an impact. Folks already knew I was a proud and loud Republican at that time. Even the kids did. I never hide who I am politically, and this cost me resources and access during Democratic regimes in power.

Global Minnesota Calls

The next evolution of my activism was an email from Global Minnesota, a nonprofit that exports citizen diplomacy from Minnesota to tackle global issues from the mundane to climate change. They said that thanks to our awesome State Department, they host nongovernmental organizations (NGOs), clergy, activists, women leaders, politicians, and even influencers to come learn what is good in America to help them overcome their local problems. They heard about my efforts from teachers who they worked with and the media. Would I be interested in speaking to their delegations? This time I did not hesitate. With any entity as prestigious as Global Minnesota, doing the work of our society, democracy, and republic, I wanted in on the process. I already had a program, formula, and methodology to do so, thanks to going into schools. Plus, I wanted a new challenge. Talking to kids who were new to this world and innocent was one thing. But talking to nuanced, experienced professionals at the heights of their careers, impacting the world at their local level—this was a new experience., I wanted to learn from them as much as to teach my methodology, program, and process of counter-ideology, which was working in America and accepted globally.

I went in fully aware that this group would be skeptical of my process, methodology, and program. I wanted to know what they thought. More important, I wanted to know what they were doing in their communities that I was not aware of, which I could add to my programs. I spoke to Africans from the Maghreb, East Africa, and West Africa. I spoke to Middle Easterners from Israel and the Gulf states. I spoke to Europeans from former Eastern Bloc nations and Western ones. I spoke to Asians from China and Thailand. I spoke to almost all nations of this world—to their activists, clergy, NGOs, politicians, government dignitaries, and even women leaders. I showcased to them the process of getting across a message relevant to their communities. I showed analytics on how many people in their countries watched my messages, and it was, for lack of resources, only in English, mostly, even though I speak and create in three languages, with Somali and Swahili being the other two from Africa. Average Mohamed may be an American at heart, but still the motherland beckons in need of help. I learned that extremism was not uniquely a problem of America. I also learned extremism was taking the forms of nationalism, white supremacy, anti LGBTQI, Islamophobia, antisemitism, and even anti-Christianity in all parts of the world, from the developed ones to third-world countries. I learned that misogyny and patriarchy were global for the women leaders of the world. I learned to understand that my approach was simplistic but revolutionary in means and effectiveness compared to what others were doing. I also learned that America is way behind in any activity to counter these issues of extremism and hate compared with other governments of the world. I had to teach others that there are Constitutional restraints as to what our government in America can do. For example, our American government cannot speak about religion. We have a separation of state and mosque in my instance. Talking religious scriptures and the teachings of Muslims to Muslims as outreach was a big no, just as it is for any other religion in America, be it church, synagogue, or even atheism. We had no minister of religion in America like they do in Africa and the Middle East.

I had to explain American culture to people from Asia, where communal understanding superseded individual understanding. I taught that, as Americans, we valued the minority. The smallest level of the minority is the individual citizen of a nation. Any infringement on their rights, except in cases of criminality or terrorism, is considered a big no in America. Our democracy and republic are built on individual rights, not societal rights. The Asians built their understanding on communal rights over individual rights, which makes it easier to manage their society. Ours was a pure "every person is a king in rights and liberties" understanding, from free speech and the right to organize to freedom of religion and freedom to associate. For the Africans, my program was something they could replicate easily and cheaply by themselves. I still have a standing order of folks who want me to train them further and get them resources to do works. The Middle Easterners are an amazing lot. Skeptics of everything, they asked questions that bordered on, "Who are you? What makes you think you can change the age-old thinking of extremism?"

I always explained that in America, we reinvent ourselves constantly, whereas they come from the old ways that remain potent today: Autocracy, kingdoms, and dictatorship, except for some lucky nations that embrace democracy. It is partly a culture of strong men, and it is strong men or families that have always led their societies for millennia. One reason why extremists easily find recruits who want to change their society is that they seek change. I advised they embrace democracy and go like Israel and Turkey, even though Israel has a Palestinian occupation problem.

Disclaimer: I am a brother of faith to Palestinians and very sympathetic to their plight. Israel chose democracy over Jewish theocracy and dictatorship despite their location near neighbors who do. Israel lives in their environment of constant war with neighbors or elements out to destroy it. No matter what, Israel chose its people's power, for the people and by the people. Israel has not just Jews as citizens but Palestinians, Druze, and others too. Who says other nations in the region cannot follow suit? The Gulf folks told me our culture is one of kings as emirs. That is their culture, and you already know I respect people's culture and understanding. I asked others about the dictatorships. Politely, off the record, they all told me that because of terrorism today, those who clamor for democracy are called terrorists by their states. They avoid clamoring for democracy in their countries but work on the margins of their societal needs.

That was then. Today some of the NGOs I met have been shuttered or hamstrung by fear of autocrats and dictators It's why I tell folks, "You just got to love America." Here, it is almost impossible to shut us up once we become activists. That does not mean our government will not try. They will try every option, but our awesome democratic Constitution was built exclusively by people who dissented and wanted dissent to be part of protected society under our laws.

The Europeans looked at us Americans as backward. Their society and governments were aggressively tackling the issue of extremism. Take, for example, Great Britain. They had a prevention program that tackled not only violent jihadi processes but right-wing and white-supremacy problems arising in society. They roped clergy, teachers, government agencies, social services, police, and civil society together in programs, methodologies, and means of resources. Their police worked with the community directly. This is controversial in some corners of their society but effective at dealing with those on the margins, if not with those already radicalized. I politely explain to our Europeans brother and sisters in democracy and republics that this is America. Programs like those in Nordic countries, France, and Great Britain would not survive a local American court in civil rights case against governmental overreach. Most don't get the level to which we Americans are deeply committed to individual rights and the limitation of our government, from the left to the right. Hence Europeans think we are backward that way.

Those from communist or dictator-controlled societies or ones where religious extremism was rampant spoke of the fear of expressing themselves. I learned not to push them in questions but to ask them off-the-record, one-on-one, what they thought when it was just me, an average guy, talking to another average gal or guy. I learned they don't speak their mind or express things like we do in America. The cultural competency to understand that is crucial to impacting their lives. I tell them what is said is for my knowledge and understanding. Take what you can get away with doing in your society from America and push the issues even if it is one millimeter at a time. One day your children will push it all the way because you laid the foundations of hope, transparency, and an end to fear of your own governments. We Americans don't fear our government. We have that right embedded into the DNA of our thinking and our awesome Constitutional rights. That's why you just got to love America.

I had been doing all this work since 2014. Thanks to our awesome state department's International Visitor Leadership Program (IVLP), I met and spoke to over a thousand NGOs, clergy, women leaders, activists, politicians, and even influencers. I made time for this process. Thanks to corporate America for giving me the flexibility to do so.

I learned a lot from this process, including that the world is facing an unprecedented surge in extremism, hate, and the antidemocratic elements of theocracies, dictatorships, and communists. Not all societies were as blessed as us Americans who were democracies with constitutions and protections. But in most of the world, the lights of hope were dimming. Average Mohamed is predicated on the concept that hope is every average person's right. That even an average person———could impact their society and country. Now I was impacting the world in meaningful ways. Each person I reached out to through the IVLP was a point of light that could, in turn, impact tens of thousands back where they came from. Many wrote back to tell me they showed the messages in their programs, from the Caribbean to Africa and elsewhere. When folks say the problems of this world are too much to bear, tell them of this Average Mohamed with no skill set who went about impacting it. Who says you cannot do the same in the name of peace and the love of all humanity? Who says you cannot stand on peace and nonviolent ways in defense of our diversity and plurality? Who says you can't impact the world for your cause? I urge you all to do it with decency and respect, within cultural understanding, with no bias or hate. Be curious and willing to learn and adapt what you learn to apply in society. Nobody can stop you. Average Mohamed did all this with just a high school education. Imagine what you can learn from a university to apply to this process.

The next step I had on my to-do list was to get better educated in means of communication to perfect my program, methodology, and process.

Chapter 6
Bush Foundation Fellowship

I applied for a Bush Foundation Fellowship. Many had urged me go to them, and my sister was a previous Bush Foundation fellow. This is an organization heavily invested in social change, equity, and expansion of opportunity to all. It was a perfect fit for me. The application process was rigorous. The first part is creating your narrative and reasoning. Once you cross the threshold of the first part, the second part is another, more detailed narrative. The last part is when three of your peers interview you to see if you are worth investing resources in.

The fellowship is one in which the individual decides what they want to do. We were awarded a $100,000 stipend to use however we wanted if the result was empowerment of our Midwest region in America. I had help from two board members to create the narrative. At this point you have already figured out I am big on ideals and values, but my writing skill is not up to par. The writings had to be concise and perfect to fit the process. I have no talent in that. I wanted the grant to advance my skill set in thinking and understanding. This process of getting resources was smooth and equal-opportunity-based. Merit works at the Bush Foundation. I was very proud to try this process to better myself and to do better for my city, state, country, and humanity.

Here I was, thinking, *Look around you. There are people who deserve this grant to do the impossible more than you do.* What did I have to offer the

Bush Foundation to merit this fellowship? Up until then I was working at the gas station as a manager, going to schools, mosques, madrasa, churches, synagogues, and even civic arenas to speak through the IVLP. I was also doing media interviews. My days and nights were full. I was indeed living up to my code of life, tiring my arms and body trying to be a square. I was trying, failing, in my eyes, because I felt I was not qualified just yet to claim the skill sets I was learning through sheer observation, research, and repetition of process. There is a knowledge that is endowed in every human being, one that comes from within. This knowledge exists based on life experiences, dispositions, and understanding. When you keep an open mind and a keen eye, you can learn from almost anything that comes your way. As my moniker, Average Mohamed, implies, I had to use knowledge based on a high school education to take on extremism and hate and promote our awesome system of governance: people's power, democracy. What I lacked is the accreditation to say I was certified to do this work. What I lacked was the more sophisticated know-how to do my works better. I felt it was time to let others come into my process to upgrade my abilities. The Bush Foundation was making that promise to select candidates.

I applied and went through the process. When asked what I would do with my $100,000, I said I would go back to being a Gopher at the University of Minnesota to get a degree. If I was practical, I would go for marketing, a business administration degree like I always wanted. That was my practical way to get from blue-collar to white-collar America. The needs of Average Mohamed were to enhance my understanding of the value of words and learn history because extremism and hate are steeped in history. What did others do to overcome that process? I also wanted to be a better connoisseur of media. How about learning journalism along the way? This was my thinking then. Should I be practical and go for my first love, capitalism, or my passion, freeing humanity from extremism and hate? Passion won, so I applied for this process, wanting to improve on delivery means of activism by upgrading my knowledge for my passion in life. I could always sell and work with the knowledge I had in me within me. The world was changing drastically, not for the good alone but for the bad too. I needed to commit to upgrading myself at the awesome University of Minnesota, a top-tier university of the world.

I succeeded in getting the fellowship in 2017. Here I was, washing toilets and serving coffee every day, doing activism every day, now adding getting educated to the process. America is a promise to us immigrants. We see what it is and what we can be given equal opportunity and access to resources. Corporate America gave me equal opportunity and access to resources to feed, clothe, and shelter my loved ones. My city, Minneapolis, and my state, Minnesota, gave me equal opportunity and access to resources to be able to live in peace and harmony if I obeyed the laws of the land and paid my taxes. America gave its citizens' welcoming disposition, love, and care. I had mentors, friends, and associates who cared about me and my progression in life. Therefore, I knew that I must be able to put back into America. I had taken so much from it and been given so much by it. I knew to love America meant service in works for America. Not just the flag-waving fanaticism and knee-jerk responses of the me-me-me culture but we-we-we, the people culture. Do not get me wrong; I believe I am vain, and even writing this book is an exercise in vanity. I did not want to just be a high school graduate. They all say education is the key to a brighter future. That is true. But that key is expensive in America. Unlike all Western first-world democracies where it is free, we pay for it ourselves, through either outright fees or indebting ourselves to the tune of tens of thousands of dollars. Just the fact that one can join in upward mobility and go back to get educated forward mobility means is a trait in America that is borne by so many. We are never content with our station in life, but that is a human trait. . We progress forward to earn more, get more, achieve more, and do more in life. This is a great country built on ideas. The ideas are a promise to all those who want what our Constitution says is the pursuit of happiness. It also says that we are all equals endowed with inalienable rights given to us by our creator. Our awesome constitution, our rule book, is our guide in our democracy and republic. Here in America, you will find others giving to all without regard to race, religion, sexuality, creed, economic class, or even nationality. I knew of these facts deeply therefore I always believed you just got to love America. Here an individual can accomplish much, given a chance to do so. . The Bush Foundation gave me that. I was now determined to go back to the University of Minnesota and go through getting a degree.

Going Back to School at the U of M at Age Forty

I had a decision to make. I could not be a full-time student, a blue-collar worker putting fifty to sixty hours a week into a job I loved as a corporate man, a father, and an activist. There are only twenty-four hours in a day, and I was pushing it, burning both sides of my candle. Something had to go. Since I could pay for my education, and my bills were not that bad, I decided my major expense was Average Mohamed, creating and disseminating messages. I had to leave working in the store, focus on getting my degree, and limited my Average Mohamed works to not being able to afford to pay for more messages. . I was struggling at this phase; our government was no help as Average Mohamed. In fact, it was a barrier, which I will explain later. I could get the taxpayers of America to pay for some of my education and use the money I saved to support my family, pay bills, and maintain the lifestyle we were accustomed to. I had four budding young children in whom I had tremendous hope and loved. I had brought them by the grace of God into this world, and it was my duty to take care of them. As a parent, this was always on my mind because I was spending so much time doing everything for income and activism for humanity. I wanted to reconnect with my family and spend more time with them, to enjoy the best part of life. It's why we do what we do as parents. I understood that all I was doing was to make this world a better place for them. They were my true wealth and legacy. Wanting a better society for them as black, Muslim, Somali, American-born, and free kids. I wanted to get to know them better. I offered my resignation from my management job. They gave me an award at our annual conference to thank me for upholding their corporate values of citizenship and profitability at the same time. I loved who I worked for because of my disposition that I am what I do. I was the best toilet washer in America bar none and offered the best customer service in America. A proud blue-collar American of the working class in our great nation. We take pride in our work, for we are who we are. No put-on or pretenses, we are just working stiffs in this country.

I had to go back to school at age forty. I felt my age in this process, sitting in classrooms with kids whose parents were from my age group and generation. My mom was ecstatic. She was so proud of me making this decision. I had misgivings. I had, up until that point, succeeded in everything I tried to do in life. Success in activism, success at work, success in raising my kids, in having a life of love, laughter, joy, and happiness in my heart. I had also successfully failed at the university level. I started my education in Virginia at George Mason University. There I failed because I was chasing fun and wasting my energies on things that led me to fail. I was young, naïve, and new in America. Everything was an adventure to me. You must understand, Virginia pride themselves on being for lovers. I was intent to be the best lover and try to chase tail, fun, and parties, not focusing on the mission to get educated. My mind was not right. I successfully failed at my first year in college. I moved to Minnesota abruptly and, at the urging of my family, tried a second time to go back to school. The University of Minnesota accepted me back in 2000. I again went back to my old habits; I mean, I was young, surrounded by all distractions. I failed again at this process. I was living an aimless life at that time. Youth believes it will live forever and get on track. That was when I decided this was not for me. That was my second failure in two good institutions of higher learning, among the best in America. I was not cut out for it then. I never went back until 2017, after getting the Bush Foundation fellowship. I was older, wiser, and more mature by now. I was less distracted, plus, I knew what I wanted out of the institution I was going back to. Maturity helped. In my earlier attempts I was not sure what I wanted to be. My family always thought that being smart, I would end up in the sciences. An engineer, a doctor, or even a lawyer for always being in a debate over something or another. That was them. I did not want to be any of those things and going to school not knowing what you want to be is bad for motivation.

The good news is, while you are taking your general requirements, you get to explore other careers that might be more suitable. You get a chance to look around you, see what others are doing, and explore to see what else is out there for you. We say in Minnesota, "Get it in where you fit in." Where you fit in is based on your passion. If I had a choice, my dream job would be to become a teacher or a businessman. My first love was built into me by my father, who taught me how to do business with just a handshake and your word. He taught me to keep my word no matter what. Once given, keep it at all costs. Coming form an age of no credit cards or credit worthiness but your face, word, service, and goods, America was different, and there were even more opportunities than in Africa. Truly a blessed country. I was forty years old, sitting in class with eighteen-year-olds and trying to get a degree. They were smarter, tougher, more ambitious, and more sophisticated about the education system than I was—rusty, old, with intermediary computer skills and a family to take care of. I had only one advantage over them: experience in life. But what does that count for? No one respects experience anymore; they respect expertise in things. This is why I knew I needed to pass for this degree this time.

The Challenges Faced and the Help by TA and Professors

One must choose which school or college to enroll in. I chose a college of liberal arts. Liberal arts is the study of humanity, whether it is communication over time or political and historical of humanity. This is a vast college where one can specialize in almost anything, from gender studies, ethnic studies, history, and journalism to political science and my favorite, philosophy. It requires a passion to want to understand the processes of the world and its thinking in both rudimentary and detailed ways, a deep exploration of the best and worst humanity had to offer. I already was an amateur historian; I love history. I was already good at communications and understood how journalism is consumed and learned from. I went that route. I learned of the great orators and communicators of the world. The Greeks of an early age, Socrates, and Plato. The lions of America, leaders whose speeches changed the world: George Washington, Abraham Lincoln, Franklin Roosevelt, John F, Kennedy, and Ronald Reagan. The activists and civil rights leaders: Susan B. Anthony, Mahatma Gandhi, the Reverend Martin Luther King Jr., Nelson Mandela, and others. I learned rhetoric and the basis of logic and reasoning in the philosophies of the world. I studied the history of nonviolent movements that espoused peace and harmony among humanity. I also studied the ugliness of humanity, including the history of African Americans in America and Jews in the world. People who faced adversity and came out intact and powerful in our society, as equals. Who faced bigotry and hate unparalleled in the annals of humanity. Yet they persevered and overcame, and some are still trying to overcome. I wanted to know what it was that made them resilient throughout time. For the African American was my elder African in America, and we needed to know what the future might learn from their past and leadership in this country we cared for. The Jews, I learned, had two thousand years of the worst history of occupation, exile, pogroms, the Holocaust, and eventually redemption. They faced and still face the most hate in the world, coming from all societies, cultures, and politics. I studied gender classes to learn about the impact of misogyny and patriarchy on women over time and their emancipation under democracy and modernity in our age, but they too have a long way to go. I learned of the LGBTQI+ community and its struggles to fit in globally and in America. I learned how to communicate better by understanding media bias and issues of inadequate representation in media—how any group different in political, race, identities, sexuality, or opinions is portrayed in the biased light of the writer's opinions rather than facts. I studied grant-writing and videography production.

    This process was a true struggle for me. I had a secret weapon on my side: my professors, teaching assistants, and career counselor. I always went back to them. Now, I am a procrastinator by nature, and lazy, I believed. But going back to school at age forty was no easy for me. Plus, my insecurities from having failed at it kept me determined to get a degree. I was always at the door of my professor, getting advice, and used my teaching assistants relentlessly. My career counselor guided me in the process of getting the exact classes I needed to meet the requirement in the fields I wanted to learn about, communications, history, and journalism.

I can wake up anytime for work and activism, but school was, aah, lazy about it, thinking I will go into the next class. I can always copy notes from another. I can do my readings too. Old habits die hard. I was content with just passing, not excelling. I was busy with my activism, which, at this juncture, was in full swing. I was running across the country and world, going to Singapore to speak and to engage in Asia, going everywhere as the demands for speaking increased tenfold. Then came the COVID-19 pandemic.

Finally Graduating in a Pandemic

When COVID hit, I was struggling in school. Then came the shutdowns. They shut down my university, the schools of my kids, the schools I was going to speak at, the mosques, the churches, the synagogues, and even civic arenas. They shut down restaurants and even parks. We were stuck in our houses. Everything went online. Education went online. I really struggled. I had four kids who I had to monitor to make sure they were getting their education, which I can tell you was the hardest thing to do. The level of knowledge we gained in this time was enormously limited. There is something to be said for a classroom atmosphere, the teacher and student relationship. The value of professors and teaching assistants can be electronically imitated but not replaced. Add the fact that I depended on many other students to help with my computer skills. Now I had to depend on my children, who could navigate it better than I could. Zoom and Microsoft Meetings became our life. My parents' health was deteriorating, and that took up even more time, taking my father, who was paralyzed and had cancer, to and from medical treatments and his basic care. As a family, we had decided a long time ago that each of us, his children, would sacrifice to take care of my father. My brother, the legislator, put his affairs in order; the mechanic and I took care of his physical and hospital needs; my baby sister gave him twenty-four-hour care; and my older sister took care of his medical insurance hurdles. We each played a role in the upkeep of both my mother and father. His health was going downhill if not for the grace of God and the awesome health care in Minnesota, especially Hennepin County Medical Center. I mean, this was an effort by all. Our doctors, nurses, nursing assistants, those who kept the hospital clean and washed it down to stop the spread of COVID. The insurance, which I told you is one reason I was loyal to the death to America, was Medicare and Medicaid that paid for my father to live in dignity without constant pain and care. That's why I just loved America and knew I had to give back to it one way or another. It is not just about taking, and America will give us everything. The people, the corporations, our county, Hennepin, the city of Minneapolis, and the awesome state of Minnesota, the greatest state in America, gave it all to us and asked for little back. Obey our laws as best as you can, pay taxes, and, as our unofficial state motto says, *be nice*. For Minnesota is *nice*.

The shutdowns were a pain in the you-know-what. I hated them but understood the reasoning. I mean, we were scared stiff by media, government, and scientists about COVID's impact. For those of us who had existing conditions, such as my father—diabetes, blood pressure, compromised immunity, and paralysis—it was a death sentence if they got COVID. I hated the shutdown, and it led to many problems. I love my family, but to spend that amount of time confined with one another, without other things to do or places to explore, was hard on all of us. I was shut in, stuck doing nothing but taking classes. Thank God I had a stipend from the Bush Foundation, but what was the rest of America doing for survival?

I spent this time reading a lot of research and ways of understanding and improving my process of programing, methodology, and presentation. But you know who else used this forced-in-place, stuck-on-internet pandemic to spread hate? The extremists. They found a community riven by conspiracies, distrust at the loss of their civil liberties due to shutdowns, and just plain boredom. The extremists had time to disseminate their ideology too. I was reading open-source, free-press media reports and researchers who were raising the alarm over it. And here I was, stuck, not out there doing work to compete against a tsunami of hate generated in America and the world. I applied for so many grants and opportunities, but those too shut down. Our government, as usual, was an alarmist but not a pragmatist in dealing with this issue of rising hate, extremism, and attacks on democracy. They still did not get it, believing power and might were enough for them, not reason and logic. Meanwhile, I was espousing peaceful, and nonviolence means of trying to engage them.

I live in beautiful Minneapolis, where George Floyd was martyred. Murdered for being wrong color because of the abuse of authority. The next thing that came was riots and mayhem. My city turned from beautiful to burned-down encampments with looters on the loose. The majority of what was burned down was owned by other poor people who had opened businesses to support their families. Working-class poor, like me, and mostly minorities. They even burned down a police station in the third precinct, where I knew the police, having worked in the neighborhood for my corporate job. Cops love donuts and coffee too. Police are good people and heroes, mostly. But this cop who murdered George Floyd was not. For what he did to George Floyd, I was speaking out but did not join in the mayhem, because I believed in social justice, not a just-us mentality but a mentality that said, "All of us."

It was just horrible and unacceptable what happened to George Floyd; we lost a life. What happened to my city is also unfair; these businesses did not deserve to be looted and burned down, creating a desert in minority neighborhoods. Those torching our cities came from across America to incite violence. They came from suburbs looking for trouble. Others were local, but the cases after the riots mostly involved out-of-towners charged with the grossest of crimes. Now is when my city needed me, my state needed me, and my country needed me to promote peace and harmony, the nonviolent ways. I was stuck in the house, afraid of COVID for my father's sake. I avoided doing anything outside. I got a job doing African American outreach for the Republican Party in Minnesota and had to give it up because of COVID. I got it and was deathly petrified, not for myself but for my aging parents. If my father contracted it, it was potentially a death sentence. I could not live with the idea that I brought home COVID because I had not done what our scientists and government suggested doing.

I graduated, and there was no festival for it. Not a party, no triumph for old heads who go back and take a chance. No graduation ceremony— I had to do it online, sending a video of me in my garments. No party, no festivities; just like in the COVID pandemic, we were resigned to being happy to being alive. I had applied for equal opportunity and access to resources to so many grants. I got nothing back in return, and again, most grants had just stopped. I did what I did best and got back to work. I became a manager at a retail store; this time I switched it up to a clothing store. Back to my blue-collar roots, I was seriously considering giving up Average Mohamed work. I had no resources, no support from government or institutions, and was demoralized by what was happening in my society, from the riots in my city to the January 6 attack on the citadel of democracy. My passion was low, and I was getting angry, feeling stuck. I considered getting a job as a communications specialist using my degree. I burnished my résumé, ready to go out and get a white-collar job. I meant to move on and just give up.

The pandemic took a lot out of us. The shutdowns shut us all down emotionally too. I thought I was alone in this, but suicides, depression, mayhem, and anger indexes in America all went up. I mean, this was tough for all of us, not just me. But we are Americans, as I kept reminding myself. We just don't give up. We never give up. We try and try and try and try again until we succeed. I tell my kids this, which I will share with you. We are Amer-*I-Can*. "I can" is part of being an American. It means we can do anything, accomplish anything, achieve anything if we keep to these core principles. If you can dream it, innovate it, work hard for it—I repeat, work hard for it—and keep your spirits up, you can at least get it in America. America is a promise to all its people bar none. The promise is our dreams and our pursuit of happiness if it does no other harm.

I promised myself two things during the pandemic. Hate and extremism were at an all-time high. From the fall of Afghanistan, the religious extremists of my faith were buoyed and, on the rise, globally. This was my reason for being an Average Mohamed. In this country, we were at each other's throats, politically. Our elite, media, and government looked like they had abandoned our long-term goals for short-term goals of power and profit. Now more than ever, we needed advocates for peace, harmony, and nonviolence. Now was the time an Average Mohamed was needed. I had just acquired the skill sets to do even better works. I came out of my COVID-induced frustrations determined to help for my God, country, and republic. Oh, it was on this time. I was smarter, better, and knew what to do and how to do it. I just needed equal opportunity and access to resources to deliver for God, country, and republic.

Chapter 7
The Awards Coming In

With every struggle comes respite, it is promised by our lord, to any human being. Here I was, still paying out of my pocket for this whole venture of trying to defeat an idea with an idea. I mean, I created messages that went global and went into the public arena to promote those values. I spent time, energy, and the limited resources of a blue-collar workingman's salary to go out and speak to the powerful, the organized, the dignitaries of foreign countries, their women leaders, and even clergy. The Average Mohamed message was simple and straightforward. If I can do this work then for my God, country, and humanity. My God I call Allah even though I am a sinner, and I will explain my sins. My country is the awesome United States of America, and I was raised by my father to value our humanity—all of it, with no exclusions or exceptions. To save lives from joining in with extremism from the get-go, at the point of inception. To compete for minds, bar none, against extremists, their barbarity and their world order that seeks to destroy what we all love: peace, harmony, society, and our democratic ideals of freedom as we practice it globally. I lived in the greatest country one could call home, where all are promised a fair shake at life. This is worth defending and promoting. Patriotism is not about what you can get out of your country but what you can do for your country, as taught by John F. Kennedy, President of the United States of America.

America took notice. I was shocked at the response I got from the media, the public, and well-wishers across the world. I was getting more invitations to speak and engage than I could handle without equal opportunity and access to resources that I had been denied by the design of others, which I will talk about later. Here I was, running around the country, going to places across like Colorado, Arizona, California, Utah, Massachusetts and Washington, D.C., to engage, thanks to a society of Americans who believed in citizen diplomacy—that diplomacy and the promotion of the American way of life and values starts with the citizen of America. That means you, me, and everyone. It means to promote the causes we feel serve our country, irrespective of our sexuality, religion, creed, race, identities, and political affiliations. I was working with Global Minnesota to do outreach. What an awesome organization; they gave me equal opportunity and access to their resources. I was not getting paid, but we made a deal. If they offered free coffee every time I came to speak, I would give unlimited speeches and trainings to all. They were true to their word, and I got unlimited coffee from them. I was true to my word, which, when given, is better than a cashier's check, based on how I was raised by my father: the handshake and word-given protocol of doing business. Once I give my word, I never take it back or go back on it. I had spoken through the association Global Ties U.S., which worked with our foreign visitors. I had done the most outreach in a short time. They noticed it, but the feedback they were getting was what shocked me in my understanding of things. I knew what I was doing was good. But in the email, I got from Global Ties U.S., I was told I was the winner of their 2018 Citizen Diplomat of the Year award.

2018 Citizen Diplomat for Global Ties U.S.

I was shocked by this. I mean, I was doing what I was doing because I was a citizen of an awesome, first-class democracy and wanted to give back. I was not getting any help with resources but self-funding the process. I was doing it for the sake of Allah, what we Muslims call *fisabilillah*. For the sake of God, save a life. The Quran teaches us that to save one life is equivalent to saving all humanity. My goal was to save first my people, the Somali youths of Minnesota, then Muslims. Then it became a global effort.

But charity begins at home. When an activist starts their path, they start local first. Here was an institution, Global Ties U.S., so grand and well-known, nominating me as their Citizen Diplomat of the Year for 2018. They would invite me to their national gathering and meeting to speak and receive an award. At first, I thought it was vanity on my part to think I was worthy of such grand recognition. After all, who am I but an Average Mohamed? A known toilet washer, activist, father, businessman, Republican, I was now a certified Citizen Diplomat of the Year. I looked at who got this award preceding me. There was Senator Fulbright, an American icon and hero; Bill Richardson, who started the United States Institute of Peace, and my favorite, Maya Angelou, the poet-activist, a woman who espoused dignity in words and prose for America. Coming from my Somali background, we are lovers of poetry. I was an avid reader of her poems. *This is vanity,* I thought to myself. Look at these heroes of America who really helped our country and humanity. Who was I to think I was an equal to them? After all, I was just an Average Mohamed.

I considered turning it down. But then I went to my think tank, my mother. I told her, "Mother, I got an award, and they want me to be their speaker at a Washington, D.C., event. What do you think?"

My mother, like all mothers, laughed at me. She said, "The world is finally recognizing you for your abilities, which I always believed in—that you were special in this world."

Nothing can be equal to a mother in this world. They are our number-one supporters and backers. Somali mothers, like all mothers, believe their children are superior and the best of the best in the world. They apply pressure and constantly admonish to do more, get more, achieve more out here in the world. This time she had gotten to see something of this process that she agreed with.

I asked my board what they thought of it—the board of the Average Mohamed Organization, which had helped without pay throughout the process. They said, "Go for it."

I told my kids I got an award. They were like, "*Aah*, we don't know what to make of it, but it looks like it is a good thing."

I went to Washington, D.C., and spoke my piece to the organization. I mean, they offered steaks and lodging; what more could Average Mohamed ask for when I was willing to work for coffee and the right to equal opportunity and access? I did what I always do, which is to spread hope and joy in works against extremism, presenting my ideas to a wider audience.

I may be an Average Mohamed, but my passion comes through in my speeches because I do the following: Talk plainly and do not pretend I am smarter than the next person or my audience (we all shit the same way). Speak in language that even a five-year-old child can understand and comprehend. Speak from my heart; I am Average Mohamed, not Saint Mohamed, not Politician Mohamed, and not a Government Spokesperson Mohamed. My fiduciary is not allegiance to one ideology, faith, or understanding or protecting the interests of the powerful. I speak from my gut, talk of what is wrong plainly and call it out. I speak in dignity, respect, and tolerance of others who don't think like I do. In Average Mohamed's case, it is extremism, hate, and promotion of democracy in good terms. I always speak in positive tones, not blame-them tones. I am an optimist and never give up on our humanity. This, I believe, is why I am a successful speaker and most sought-after. I speak truths to those who want to hear them. I got awarded, and my vanity level increased. I felt the rewards of all the struggle and work I had put in.

Then came the next shocker. The awesome state department nominated me their Citizen Diplomat of the Year for 2020. This time I was thoroughly shocked.

2020 State Department Award

Apparently, someone put my name up and asked for people to vote on it. I was elected by state department employees during the Trump administration, by their contractors and vendors, and even by dignitaries as the most important citizen diplomat in America for the year 2020, in the middle of a pandemic. This was the United States Department of State. I consider this agency to be the excellence of America. I mean, in Africa, I saw what USAID did to feed my people in hunger and starvation. They are doing it now too. I was in Africa to see what the state department does for the cause of peace. They talk constantly to just about anybody to promote peace, democracy, rights, freedoms, equality, and liberty across the world. These were my heroes, all of them, from their guards and the marine detachment to diplomats and aid-workers. These people recognized me as the most important facet of American foreign policy goals in citizen diplomacy. Now I was getting big-headed, no longer just an Average Mohamed.

This time I did not hesitate but was humbled by this process. I accepted the award from an undersecretary of the state department via Zoom. This was at the height of COVID. I didn't get my steak and cheese from them, but I got the award. I brought my mother and children along this time. I wanted my children, born in America, to know that with hard work and love of country one can achieve anything here. I wanted my mother there because she was and still is my biggest supporter. When I get down, she brings me up, and when I have doubts, she clears them for me. This illiterate woman who learned through American adult education how to write her name in English was my backbone. My children were my true wealth and inheritance for my country. I wanted them to see citizenship and what it means to be an American. Can you imagine a black man, a Muslim, foreign-born, a known Republican, being the Citizen Diplomat of the Year 2020? A toilet washer by trade, now a university graduate, a father, and an activist on his own dime for lack resources, which were denied by others' designs at that time? This was based on national-security paranoia, which I will explain later.

This was my American government—well, an agency, the awesome, beloved state department—saying, "We value you enough, Black man, Muslim, foreign-born, even a Republican, to make you the Citizen Diplomat of the Year for America." This was vanity for me, but it was what I needed at that time, physically caring for an invalid father whose health was deteriorating dramatically. Dealing with COVID shutdowns that stopped our Average Mohamed outreach. Dealing with the inability to get resources beyond Minnesota-based organizations like our proud police department of Saint Paul and the Metropolitan Regional Arts Council (MRAC). I mean, the Average Mohamed was getting rejection upon rejection upon rejection for access to resources from all other sources. This was not natural, and I will explain why later.

I had never felt pride as I did when getting these awards. It was not what I expected or even sought. I just wanted to protect what's ours: life, liberty, rights, and the pursuit of happiness for all, starting with Somali people, then our American people, then humanity. Here were institutions of respect and honor saying, "We value you." I don't cry often, but I cried by myself after both ceremonies. I cried because of the struggles I was facing and how I was beginning to see light at the end of the tunnel. If you ever hear anybody disrespecting our awesome state department, tell them this Average Mohamed story. They, unlike one agency in America, offer equal opportunity and access to resources inshallah in the future. The state department gave awards to a Black man, a Muslim, foreign-born and a Republican, just like it would to any other out here in America. The speeches for both awards are on my YouTube page, Average Mohamed, of course; you can watch them both. Global Ties is an awesome institution that promotes American ideals, and I am deeply proud of their recognition too.

Are you beginning to understand what it means to dream, innovate, and work hard? That in America there is a fundamental understanding of merit? When you merit them, you get awards like I did, just an Average Mohamed. Not rich, just a blue-collar worker who got educated but still, in his heart, will always be a blue-collar man of America, a toilet washer and coffee server no matter what award I get. I keep to my roots as an immigrant who got his American dream through sheer hard work and perseverance.

Good is not perishable in America. America values good and exalts it to a level beyond the ordinary. I am a living witness of that aspect of our awesome America. It's why I always say you just got to love America.

Here you can do the impossible in a short time when you are determined. I was determined to do good for God, country, and humanity. My country was responding in recognition to my works in real time. Loyalty to this country is not fanaticism, flame-throwing, or radicals trying to change it, but patriots determined to go to work and win minds for the causes of this awesome America. One mind at a time, one soul at a time. Is this not the truth of my experience so far?

I'm not saying there have been no struggles. But there is more good in America than there is bad. There is more love in America than there is hate. Good does not perish easily in America. Average Mohamed's experience is proof of it. I was living up to my awesome Constitution in America, pursuing my happiness. That happiness is freedom for all. Is this not a great country, one that deserves your understanding and appreciation? The last bastion of free mankind? That, in essence, is our Average Mohamed message, not just to Americans but to humanity globally.

Chapter 8
What We Face Today in America

Transitioning to a More of Mission Value Expansion

"What next?" has always been my attitude as I approach life. The Muslim community accepted my messages—not all, but most. There was one constant complaint about my messages: "Why don't you defend us and our community, then, from non-Muslim aggression?"

In my speaking engagements, one constant theme is Muslims complaining of outright Islamophobia and surveillance in their community. For the surveillance component, I told them my staple message. If you are good and do good, you have nothing to worry about. As for Islamophobia, I explained that because an Average Mohamed exists and goes into spaces that other Muslims don't get access to, we are spreading the concept of peace. Islam is peace, and that has a knock-on effect on Islamophobia in our communities. Our goal was to create an atmosphere of communion between the faiths of Christians, Muslims, Jews, and others, who do not believe. We are to defeat the abomination of extremism.

They always countered, "All we see is you going and labeling violent jihadis. What about our causes, Average Mohamed?

What about the issues I was asked about by others? They were right because up until then my focus had been on these nihilist butchers of humanity with their wanton violence and denial of the existing global order. The post-World War II order that America had created with allies. The order of rules and relationships between societies and nations led by America and allies. This order was built on the backs and blood of those who fought another generation of fascists and dictators during World War II.

"Are we, humanity, to go back to dictatorships of theocracy in Muslim communities?" I would argue. "Have we not witnessed the growth of human freedom in the last eighty years under this global order?" It may not be just, and it is predicated on the greed of the powerful, but it has tremendously helped the cause of peace in the world. As a species, we humans had not evolved beyond war and strife. But the American-led global order let many countries rise into creating conditions for freedom to prosper under democratic norms. I may be biased but think of it. No major global wars in the period after the creation of an American order by major powers in the world. Many civil conflicts, a lot of independence movements, but no major, catastrophic wars among the major powers of the world, giving room for so many to come out from under war into prosperity. The global index of growth and improving human conditions is a testament to that and why I believe in an American-led order of global freedom.

Yet the world moves on, and gradually, this is being challenged. The greatest challenge of our time then was violent jihadists who had a political power-grab system. Theirs was a tactic of using violence and terror to force the people to submit to their order of men. Only men were to control power. No women were allowed. These men speak for God through their narrow understanding that to question them is to question God. In essence, they set themselves up for absolute power over our Muslim *ummah*. They figured if they could kill Christians, Westerners, and Muslims who were different from them, the upheaval it caused would create chaos, and from that chaos they could go about building their new society: a theocracy built on brutality and subjugation of differences, be they in religion, sexuality, race, creed, or understanding. I could not imagine being free in that society. I could not accept their barbarity. Those that wantonly kill men, women, and children will not bring about any good for men, women, and children, no matter what their cause. The proof is in their methodology.

We had created messages in support of women's rights as human rights that went viral. Average Mohamed went against slavery, which was being reintroduced by violent jihadis in this century, and promoted peace and anti-extremism. Yet criticism by others was valid. Here I was, focused on taking on violent jihadis while my own community was telling me, "You need to come forward about Islamophobia and the issue of surveillance unleashed on our communities."

The Jewish community took me in, especially their leaders and civil rights organizations. They explained the history of antisemitism, and later, at the University of Minnesota, I learned about it more deeply. For over two thousand years, their story has been one of exile, forced repatriations, slavery, pogroms, genocide, the Holocaust, and refugees. They finally formed a country again, called Israel, only to face permanent war and existential survival as a nation. Here in America, we were both minorities as Muslims and Jews. Here in America, we learned we had a common enemy, for antisemites are the same as Islamophobes in their understanding of their global standing. They both share a superiority complex that directly denies us as a people.

I was already black. I knew and understood that racism was the original sin in America. I was blessed not to have experienced outright racism, but did, like all black people in America, know that it was just around the corner when it came to resources, equality, and those who have power over us. The black kids told me repeatedly that racism was impacting them negatively, that I needed to speak up on it too.

"What about us?" the LGBTQI+ community of students asked me. "Here you are talking about issues of extremism. We face ostracization, not being accepted, and never being allowed peace of mind, based on others' perceptions." Violent jihadis were throwing LGBTQI+ people from rooftops in Iraq and Syria. In some countries, they faced punishments from jail to hanging for the crime of existing. In America, bias still existed against their community.

The Christians asked me again and again why the terrorists were committing genocide against Christians in the Middle East, Asia, and Africa. "We see you fighting for peace, but what about us? Is this Islam, and what are you doing about it, this anti-Christianity spreading across the Muslim world?"

I was having heady conversations across America and the world, learning that my mission value was limited. That the problems that underlined our society were complex and needed a more complex response. I sat down with my board, and we devised what should we do next. What were our mission values?

It all came down to a concept. The concept is as American as apple pie. Diversity is our strength. What does diversity mean, then? It means the acceptance of all. No matter what our core beliefs are, we should accept the other for who and what they are. The Jew, Muslim, Christian, Black, Brown—other races, sexualities, creeds, religions, and other markers. If we are going to live in our society as a free people, then we must learn to accept one another. The value we espouse is *love one another*. It is not good enough to tolerate one another. What humanity sought was respect, dignity, freedom, rights, and liberties to live in what our awesome constitution called the pursuit of happiness, if it does no other harm. This was lofty goal, but then, again, it came down to, "How do we go about doing so?" What can an Average Mohamed do to impact this discourse globally? For now I was a global-impact organization. Self-funded, mostly, but I was having that kind of impact by reaching millions through social media, speaking engagements, and mainstream media.

The Reasoning Why

There had to be a reason why God made me hear all these stories of hate in our societies. For the Somali kid who is called *Midgan* or *Jerer*, meaning "untouchable," or nappy-head in our Somali community, trying to understand what his or her heritage has got to do with being ostracized and seen as lesser by our own Somali peoples, racism and inequality are not just a white person's problem. They also exist within our own black and colored communities. Africans complain of African Americans' disrespect, and African Americans believe Africans think less of them, both of which things are true. Do we tackle that too? Why should the Jewish community face hate for being Jews? Can we be the ones who break the cycle or at least help in doing so? What about Christians who are afraid to venture out of America for missionary missions to get souls because of terrorism against their faith? What to do for my LGBTQI+ community members, whom all are against for their sexuality? I was just an Average Mohamed. Did I need to expand my process to include these communities and issues too? I had doubts about this process, and while at the university I made sure I learned about these issues firsthand through readings and research. I learned of the Stonewall movement of the gay community in America and their transitioning from hiding to coming out into the public domain. I learned of the hate they faced and how they went about setting up movements to fight for their equality in America.

I visited the Anti-Defamation League in New York to learn more about antisemitism and went into synagogues in beautiful Minnesota to learn what it is to be a Jew in the world today. I was already black, steeped in the teaching of my heroes. You must understand, I am a tribal child of the Somali people. A Black man who came to America. Here in America, our elder blacks are the African Americans, the descendants of slaves. They have lived in America for longer and understand the true dynamics of this system better than us, and we learned to defer to them. I learned about their heroes, now all our heroes, such as Booker T. Washington, Sojourner Truth, Harriet Tubman, and others, like my favorite, Frederick Douglass. Then I came to learn of the Reverend Martin Luther King Jr.'s movement of Southern Baptists churches, the Freedom Riders, the sit-ins, and the mass movement to emancipate themselves through nonviolent, peaceful means. And my president at that time was a Black man, President Barack Hussein Obama, whom I had voted and campaigned against twice as a Republican but who still gave me hope that America would keep on reinventing itself over time to be more inclusive in freedoms, liberty, and rights. I went into churches and spoke to missionaries about the challenges they face. I learned that security is now a component of their missionary work around the world. Can you imagine just speaking of faith, of Christianity, and requiring personal protection from armed men and women to spread the gospel?

I was learning because I wanted to understand. I was biased on some issues. For instance, I never thought America had a systemic problem with racism. I believed it was an individual problem, with the systemic part largely muted in America. But I also learned, talking to youths, that their reality is one in which the scorn that covets their skin color is permanent and abrasive. Being raised in Africa, I did not experience systemic racism. Plus, being raised a Somali, we are taught from a young age who and what we are: equals to all in humanity and blessed to be Muslims. So Islamophobia did not scare us, because we believed that we worshipped an awesome God called Allah and we were on the right path.

All this took me by surprise. Here I was, proudly a protagonist for America. But within America lay a rot that was manifesting itself. I watched the news, shocked, as racists came out into the open and marched in Charlottesville, in Virginia, the state of lovers, shouting "the Jews will not replace us!" and holding torches like the Nazis of the past. I understood then that those who hate the Jews have no love for Blacks or Muslims or the LGBTQI+ community and were not Christians as they claimed.

Then there was a shooting in Christchurch, New Zealand, where a guy walked into a mosque and shot Muslims in savagery. He had even written a manifesto, which other terrorists are using to copycat that effort because of Islamophobia. I knew then that this would be my next challenge to tackle.

Using the Existing Tools
The tools I had were my voice, imagination, innovations, and spirit. As a proud blue-collar worker, I had some money I could use to fund the

process. I had to learn to create. I learned I knew what I knew. Once I knew what I knew about the issues, then I could impact them. The "how" is a message: a video, an article, a speech, or an engagement in media, on social media and in civic arenas. This was work that didn't pay, but by now you know that to go about doing works for God, country, and humanity, I sacrifice everything: time, energy, resources, and even peace of mind. I had popular-culture tools and messaging means available. I learned the hot topics and learned how to message against them.

We had governments across the world grappling with these problems. Their solution was persuasion, which failed because these segments of populations do not believe in governments. The use of legal means succeeds in suppressing the more violent components of antisemitism, Islamophobia, anti-Christianity, racism, and anti-LGBTQI+. The good guys and gals of the world are hard at work in government agencies, disrupting processes before harm comes. But they send culprits to jail, which then becomes a breeding ground for recruitment into extremism. It was a whack-a-mole process. The level of hate has skyrocketed in this world. "Help us," governments from across the world urged us. Average Mohamed was predicated on helping our democracies and republics of the world, bringing about the issue, "Whom do we target, just democracies and republics or the entire human race on this globe?"

That was the question I pondered the most. If you look at hate, it is a tactic terrorists and bigots use to gain power. "Divide you all and rule in the chaos" was their strategy. What did they hate the most? . In essence, the enemy's target was the American model of democracy as it exists and is espoused today. We are not all the way there yet but have come a long way. What they hated the most was people deciding their own destiny as espoused by Abraham Lincoln, a government of the people, by the people, for the people. People's power was anathema to those who espouse hate. That means that we had to promote people's power. The only true means of people's power are democratic and secular because God was separated from the state. The theocrats wanted to shove their understanding of God on all, regardless of their beliefs or nonexistent beliefs. The dictatorship of faith was preordained on all, whereas the state is the arbiter of faith—not God only but the state, you, and then God. In essence, the state becomes God, representative, unquestionable, and saintly.

Now, the problem with this is that God is pure. God is beyond earthly ways. Yet politics is impure, in fact downright corrupt, globally; it does not matter if it's a first-world or third-world nation. People are disgusted by the discourse of the other side, whatever side you are on politically. We will never, as a species, agree to one form of politics or understanding. Opposition is needed, as are imagination, innovation, and the means to deal with modern global problems without the passion of faith alone but also with reason, logic, and science. That is what is denied by theocratic systems. The free-for-all discourse that comes from people's power. Not that people's power has all the right answers, but a plurality of answers is expressed, organized for, and promoted freely for the masses to decide which path to go down. Under theocracy, that is not a choice.

Next is communism. Here, order is dictated by the party. The party is jealous of any entity being elevated above its doctrines. That means God too. In fact, they call religion, all religions, the opium of the masses. In essence, communists consider your worship of God to be a drug addiction. Think about it. Hence, belief in communism socialist ways is the discourse the real drug addiction is power for their party and ideals. Absolute power by a party over everything in your life. You don't vote for your leaders; they are appointed for you, just like in a theocracy. A committee of individuals has vetted them for their veneration of the party, and only those loyal to the party are allowed to run your society. Believe in God? Bad luck—you are not included. Believe in people's power of choice? You are in jail. Believe in human rights for all? You are also in jail. The order is top-down, just as in dictatorships. The system of dear leaders. Disagree or oppose the dear leaders and you end up dead. And all things done by the communists and theocrats are part of the dictatorship process. Self-appointed leaders, they are considered demigods of power, not to be questioned, petitioned, or even challenged for that power. In essence, the human spirit is under their domain in their society of the few, for the few, by the few in power.

This was the rising arc of dictatorship, communism, and theocracy in this century, during our lifetime, in this world built on hate of others. The absolute hate of freedoms, rights, liberties, and opportunity for all based on their narrow understanding as to who was eligible for them. That does not include the free-spirited people who cherish freedom in this world, in democracies and republics of people's power. I understood that hate is the basis of this power. Absolute power is corrupting and will lead to worse outcomes for humanity. I preferred a place where I could vote in freedom and vote in who I wanted freely. Where even I, an Average Mohamed, can have a voice to speak my piece in freedom. Where dissent is considered patriotic and an important part of our society, including the freedom to worship how we see fit to worship if it does no harm to another. Freedom of religion, freedom of speech, freedom to associate, and freedom not to live in fear of our government or the powerful. Let them fear our people's might and power. The individual is the smallest form of minority that exists in this world. You are a minority of one, irrespective of your values, understanding, and principles. You are important, and if we protect you, the individual, we protect me, another individual. The concept espoused by dictatorships, communists, and theocrats for the greater good is only benevolent to themselves and their power. I chose to expand my mission goals to include the promotion of democracy against communism, dictatorship, and theocrats.

The Types of Hate and Extremism

My new mission value and core process was now defined. A counter-ideology organization that promotes democracy in rights, liberties, and freedoms; fights extremism of religious, racial, and ideological natures; and stands against hate, antisemitism, racism, Islamophobia, anti-Christianity, and anti-LGBTQI+. I love to expand my challenges in life and knew that with my education from the awesome University of

Minnesota, diligent research, and analysis from open-source free media and researchers of credibility, I had a clear understanding. There was knowledge that came from within me and knowledge I sought from outside. I am always learning, questioning, understanding, and then applying processes to works. They say you stop learning when you are dead. I wasn't dead; in fact, I felt younger because I had found my passion and destiny in life. I was busy working it out, figuring things out, and knew what I had to do and how to do it to win minds against those I espoused against.

Who are these who I espouse against? The communists, dictators, and theocrats coming after your and my democratic way of life. Why go after them? Because this is a monkey-see-monkey-do world. What they do in their societies will get exported to us here and your country eventually, one way or another. It is our freedom that so many generations bled, fought, and died for that we stand to lose. If we don't stand up today for our values, all of us, each in their own way, we will find, in the words of President Ronald Reagan, that "Freedom is never more than one generation away from extinction. We didn't pass it to our children in the bloodstream. It must be fought for, protected, and handed on for them to do the same, or one day we will spend our sunset years telling our children and our children's children what it was once like in the United States, where men were free."

I don't want to say I came to America only to see democracy fail globally because of the rising arc of dictatorship, communism, and theocrats coming at us. Let's, then, go after them too, using our existing freedoms of speech and other nonviolent, peaceful means: the Average Mohamed way, which I learned from others in the history of our existence.

We would also fight extremists, be they the international kind, like violent jihadists, or domestic terrorists, like the ideological ones that stormed the citadel of democracy in on January 6, 2020, or the ones who marched in Charlottesville, Virginia, or the QAnon conspiracy theorists, or the far-leftists that torched our cities, such as antifa. Those with fascist tendencies who claim to fight fascists.

Hate is the basis of this process of death. Hatred of Jews, Blacks, Muslims, Christians, and LGBTQI+, which leads to more deaths. Hate manifesting itself in mass shootings of synagogues, churches, mosques, temples, LGBTQI+ facilities, black, brown, and Asian people.

Why Fight Hate?

Why even bother, especially on my own dime? Because I believe in my God even though I am a sinner, not a saint, with bad habits that lead to sin. I believe in my country, America, and want to be the voice of it in spirit and values, even if I am an Average Mohamed. I believe in my humanity and want humanity to live free from the despotic powers of communism, dictatorship, and theocracy, free from extremists and hate. I can dream for myself, for I am a very selfish human being. I want for myself all those things above. Why, then, should I not serve myself, my interests, and in the process serve country and humanity? For it is in their interest too.

I would be doing so in the footsteps of many, the known and un-known of this world. The average people who pushed these values one millimeter at a time, against all odds, to get us to where we are today. Democracy is a hand-me-down society in which strangers hand down values and understandings over generations to other strangers to expand the horizon of the human spirit and freedom. Why shouldn't I, or maybe you, not be the one doing so? And if you are going to do it, do so with respect, dignity, and honor to our God, country, and humanity, what-ever god you believe in or do not believe in, without shoving it down everybody else's throats. Your country deserves you to stand up for it. Mine is America, home of the brave and the free. It really is to be free; one must be brave to espouse freedom. Freedom is not free, for over a million veterans died for that freedom we so cherish today. Millions upon millions, from those shackled in slavery to the women told go barefoot and the LGBTQI+ community, were told hide and were raided, yet they always marched, petitioned, and organized for what you see in America today. Who said you are not the one to take our freedom even further?

I am very selfish as a person. This freedom I want for myself and my loved ones, friends, peoples, and society. Hence an Average Mohamed going into the arena armed with the words of Theodore Roosevelt, who talked of "the man in the arena" during a citizenship speech: "It is not the critic who counts, not the man who points out how the strong man stumbles or where the doer of deeds could have done them better. The credit belongs to the man who is actually in the arena, whose face is marred by dust and sweat and blood; who strives valiantly; who errs, who comes short again and again, because there is no effort without error and shortcoming; but who does actually strive to do the deeds; who knows great enthusiasms, the great devotions; who spends himself in a worthy cause; who at the best knows in the end the triumph of high achievement, and who at worst, if he fails, at least fails while daring greatly, so that his place shall never be with those cold and timid souls who neither know victory nor defeat".

I always say believe in America, if not you who then will do so. Fail if you must but become the man or woman in the arena for a worthy cause. I am not afraid to fail, that is my secret to success in all things worthwhile.

Which Hate Brings the Most Backlash?

I went about creating messages espousing my core mission values. It was not all great reception, because what was I doing, going into the public arena where values were already entrenched? People believe what they believe but are open to persuasion. The kids, mostly, because they haven't formulated their understanding of the world yet but have ideas about it. My role as Average Mohamed was to present our collective values to this population across the world. For it takes an idea to defeat an idea. Like a bed of roses, there are thorns that prick us too.

Of all the values I espouse, the one that gets me the most vitriol is the LGBTQI+ issue. Man does this issue galvanize open hostility and opposition. I understand why. I was once a homophobe in my ways, raised on religion and African culture that taught us clearly that homosexuality or other sexuality is deviant from the path of God. I still cannot walk away from my faith-based understanding of this ideology, as hard as I try, and I am a moderate in thinking. What about those I love who feel the same way? I am at the 1950s America level of understanding LGBTQI+ issues, as they were of the black people in America. At that time, whites accepted that blacks needed equality and freedoms, but "not just now, and don't move into my neighborhood or country club or associations." I had to relearn what I knew. Nature did this for me. My coworkers were gay men and lesbians. They had signs on their desks and cars that said "all are welcome;" they accepted all even though they faced hate for who they were. My neighbors, who were flying the gay flag, had, during Ramadan, a sign that said, "We wish our Muslims blessed Ramadan."

Here were a people I detested and opposed their rights to come into society, not only standing up for me but also standing up for my faith. What right did I have to judge my coworker who had a family and found love in another? Who gave me the right to shove my understanding down their throats? Did that mean that I was a bigot? Yes. They say religion is tolerant of many things but sin. I do not want to change your religious beliefs. That is not my mission value. What I knew I had to do was change the optics of freedom, expanding it to include the LGBTQI+ community. How can my freedom be predicated on them not having theirs? Who decides who gets freedoms to live their lives as they see fit in their reality? What gave me the right to deny another that right?

What did it for me was when I saw ISIS throwing gay men off of building roofs. That galvanized my thoughts. I get the most hate and denial of opportunity for speaking about LGBTQI+ issues in my works. Second is the support of Jews. I am a brother to the Palestinian cause. I believe their occupation and subjugation are inhumane and contrary to freedom. But I will not turn a blind eye to antisemitism. Many out here who are Muslims today are beginning to understand that, thanks to the Abraham Accord among some Arab nations and the Jewish state of Israel. Some think if you defend Jewish statehood, you are abandoning the Palestinian cause of freedom and statehood. That is a false narrative. Israel is a democracy, and the Jews feel they are under existential threat by all in this world. Based on their history and understanding of it documented for over five thousand years their history. To make Jews put down their arms one must espouse peace to them. Why not defend them in our humanity and keep on asking them for the freedoms of the Palestinians too? We can do both at the same time, not vilifying and ostracizing the Jew and Israel. That has not worked in over sixty years of doing so. Peace and mutual defense of one another is the path forward to real peace, I believe. I also believe that one day we shall see a two-state solution in the holy lands. That is the hope I have for my Palestinian brothers and sisters. That is in line with what Americans and most of humanity believe in. But the Islamists, nationalists, and leftists come at me on this issue.

The third most hate I get is from far right-wing Republicans. These folks hate Muslims with a passion. They hate people of color. The fact that I stood up and went to global media saying Islam is peace and being a Black man really made them angry. They go to lengths to insult my religion, my noble prophet, and even my race. I have been told all they needed to learn about Islam was September 11, as if nineteen men led by mad, evil men—and they were all men—validated the beliefs of almost 1.8 billion believers. I got so much hate from them, insulting my intelligence calling me a fifth column trying to bamboozle Americans into believing Muslims when we were the enemy undercover, pretending to be accepting but radicals in our heart, faith and understanding. Some even said. "You can never be an American."

The fourth hate I got was from the far left, especially when they found out I was a Republican activist too. This riled them up. The questions kept on coming. "You espouse peace, diversity, and tolerance yet are a Republican? It cannot be." One photo of me welcoming Trump with other Muslims went viral. I had a sign that said Muslims for Trump.

Now let me digress and tell you my President Trump story. We went to the airport to welcome Trump in Minnesota, where he was to speak at the hanger. In his rambling speech, he said, "Can you believe they brought Somalis to Minnesota?" And the crowd booed. Here I was, a

Muslim welcoming our Republican nominee and a Somali, and Trump was basically saying that. And that picture was posted on social media that same day. It went viral and got over ten thousand comments on my Facebook page. I even had to take it down. The cancel culture took effect immediately after that. Many just canceled my speaking engagements, projects, and their associations with me. Now, Trump is Trump, shoot first and let others deal with the consequences. I was a Republican all right, and that meant Republican support for Republican ideals of small government, more freedom for the citizen, and even a strong military. I was a Republican because of George W. Bush, "Dubya," whom I still love to this day. The man was a lion. But I was always a moderate in my politics. Here, my party gave us a Muslim ban along with vitriol that was ammunition for this far left and their cancel culture. I learned firsthand that my liberal brothers and sisters are liberal if you agree with them, illiberal in ways when you show a different understanding. The fact that I was a Republican in a state that was heavily Democratic made life very difficult for me in my beautiful cities dominated by Democratic voters. Even local government agencies avoided us for it, and they were supposedly for all the people.

I am still a Republican to date, espousing and working for Republican ideals across America. I even created a political action committee, Republicans People of Color (RPOC), to espouse moderate Republican values after being frustrated by how ineffectively mainstream Republicans did outreach to our communities. Hate me or love me for it, this is my right and freedom. I will not ask any permission to do what I want to do politically in this world. No more than I asked any for the right to become an Average Mohamed.

The Death Threats , Hate Mail, and Cancel Culture

The one hate that shook me a bit, for a moment, was the death threats and promises of a good beating by some youths. When I started posting our videos on social media, there was a cadre of folks who followed me on my site. Some even had the ISIS or al-Shabab or al-Qaeda flag. I was curious as to what they would say about the products I was putting up. They said nothing for the first few months. I was ecstatic about it because here I was, reaching the very same community I wanted to reach. Then some stopped following me. I was happy about the fact that even my religious claims of messaging were beyond question. I was always worried about that aspect. It is one thing to be passionate about a cause, but we are not entitled to our facts on faith. My process of seeking knowledgeable people and research of ulama and imams who espoused those values ("ulama" being scholars and "imams" clergy) panned out.

Then came the death threats. ISIS was the first. "I will find you and get you." Then more death threats from al-Shabab and al-Qaeda. I was worried. My family panicked. My wife was distraught about it for the sake of my kids. There is a reason why I don't use names in this book. Those who want to harm me, my family, and my associates need no names to find us. I value human life above all. The greatest liberty we have as human beings is life itself. This is the gift that no one has the right to take away. Because no one in our humanity can give it back. Money comes and goes; everything else is transient, but life is one thing we have until it ends. I wanted to die of old age, fat with grandchildren and great-grandchildren. But here I was getting death threats via phone calls and on social media sites. Others in the know would come up to me and say, "This so-called hard-liner imam called you out as a blasphemer and apostate." The extremists, when they cannot defeat your ideas, use this ideology of blasphemy as their last recourse. If they call you an apostate, then your life is free for them to kill and take.

I sat down and thought. Who did religious nuts call blasphemers and apostates in the history of mankind? Galileo, for saying the earth is round. Anybody promoting democracy is considered an apostate. Anybody who believes in freedoms, liberty, and justice for all, no exceptions and no exclusions, is an apostate. Any who believes in women rights and liberties is an apostate, especially if they are not barefoot and pregnant and secluded. Then all government officials are considered apostates, which is good for killing them. I am in good company. I did not and will never go against the religion, any religion, or espouse what is not in it as if the religion mandates it. If it does not, I will say so clearly and use nonreligious logic and reasoning. Even when I espouse democracy and speak against hate of LGBTQI+ people, I don't use religion; this is our secular thinking process. Our humanity is not just religion for me. It is our reality too.

The media picked up on the death threats too. I got asked, "Are you worried about it?" I would usually smile and laugh about it.. My coworkers worried harm would come their way because of my works. My family and friends urged me to get protection, to buy a gun and train in defensive means. I eased my coworkers' worries, and they, especially my corporations, showed love and understanding. I explained to my wife, jokingly, "I am insured with life insurance." My children would be taken care of when and if I went. I did not buy a gun for protection because I had small kids and was petrified the weapon would get into their hands, along with another reason I will explain later in the book. I changed nothing of my habits, nothing of my ways. I did not stop go-ing out for speaking engagements. The main reason for this was belief. I believe no one out here is promised a tomorrow. By the grace of God, we survive day-to-day and the next day. By his mercy, we live. When and if my time comes to go, I cannot add a second of life to what God has ordained. Nor can any take a second of my life that God has not ordained. I will live a full life with my works. And if I save a life, and I am saving and reaching millions at a time from the error of hate and extremism, and for democracy. Gradually, then, I am doing God's work, and that is mercy. That means I have a slight shot at going to heaven even though I am a sinner. The greatest thing one can do is not to live in fear. As the words of a man in wheelchair at the height of power in a previous age said, "We have nothing to fear but fear itself" (President Franklin Roosevelt). I had nothing to fear but fear itself.

Here I was, vocal and active globally, and some kids didn't like what I said and was doing. I had gone to the court steps in the Minneapolis federal court building and spoken up about the biggest ISIS case in America. I said I had heard from witnesses what they said, how they plotted and planned, in their own voices. Yes, an informant was paid an enormous amount to get that information. But we do have a problem with our youths if this is to be believed in defense of the good guys and their case. The kid's friends and associates came to my gas station on three separate occasions and threatened that if they ever caught me outside, they would beat the hell out of me. I did what I always do: smile, laugh, and walk away from it. If I was due a beating for speaking truths—which I knew was making me unpopular among the far right, the far left, Islamists, violent jihadists, and kids who were just angry and looking for someone to punish for their friends' misdeeds and did not want me to speak at all—this was a choice I accepted. You see, I believe with all my heart that the world is a hard place as it is. I am kindhearted; I will smile, laugh, have joy and love in my heart and go about doing my works. Hate me or love me; it does not matter. I care less for fame or infamy than for spreading my message and understanding for the betterment for your humanity. Speak in truths, always, no matter whom it offends. My truths, not necessarily what you will agree with. After all, you have your own truths, reality, and understanding. But together, the truth lies in between us both, and I am willing if you are willing to share my truths and learn your truths. The give-and-take of life, the yin and yang of it. If harm comes my way, so be it. But expect me to speak my truths. The world majority was accepting and celebrating my truths as an Average Mohamed.

Today we see teachers, doctors during the pandemic, and now even federal agents and police getting death threats just for doing their works. Politicians the most, especially the women politicians of the world. We are still a patriarchy, a world with some misogynists. My advice is to buy life insurance and change nothing. You have nothing to fear but fear itself. Once you submit to fear, they win, period. We all lose then because after you, we are next. Is that not terror and why I created the moniker of Average Mohamed to fight it? We are, after all, the free people of the world. You must be brave to live free. That is the American way, if you read and understand our history. What Reverend Martin Luther King Jr., Mahatma Gandhi, George Washington, Nelson Mandela, and every activist in the world had to come to think of and live with.

Do you not think they did not be afraid in their hearts yet became lions for their cause? The cause of freedom.

If you feel the need to serve humanity, to be a protagonist for good, expect the bad to react and want to finish you off one way or another. That has always been the cost of freedom. In all ages, that price has never changed. Very few get to see their works fulfilled the way they wanted. Many will lose lives over it. But most humanity will gain from it. That is our Average Mohamed dream. I hope to see old age, fat and happy, *inshallah*, if God wills it, and rooting for all out here doing their millimeter push for humanity's freedom, liberty, justice, and rights.

Chapter 9

Challenges Faced

Mental Illness Is No Barrier to Success

I do suffer from bipolar disorder. I was diagnosed in Minnesota. The doctor, or rather, psychiatrist, said it was genetic. I am not big on or an expert in science but learned the following to be true. I was suffering from mistrust. I did not trust my government after September 11.

Let me explain. I was smoking marijuana at that time. My biggest regret in life was ever picking up a joint. I lost a decade of ambition, work, and good jobs because of it. I was smoking the Mary Jane while working and partying and chasing tail. I partied hard. I never believed in hard drugs. Anything chemical scared me for good reason, because in my time, we called those that did pills or smoked anything synthesized fiends or crackheads, addicts. What marijuana did was to limit me. I had no idea how much until I quit after smoking it for almost ten years. This drug—and it is a drug—is not meant for everyone. I know people who use it to function in work and school. For some it is medicine. For me it did the opposite. It brought about being lazy and unambitious, just happy all the time but with no focus. I was already a procrastinator, but this drug made me a super procrastinator. Everything seemed so far away. I had a do-it-tomorrow mentality.

Now, I also drank alcohol at that time. I chewed on khat, a leafy plant that is used traditionally across Africa and the Middle East. These were all-natural and illegal in America, except alcohol. I was not an addict or a casual user but regular casual user. I smoked regularly around that time. Add the fact I smoked cigarettes and chewed tobacco and smoked cigars. I was a man of habits. I always worked hard but was never focused when I was using the marijuana. This and chasing women are my sins.

Why am I telling you of this? Because those habits led to me being profiled. I was always opinionated and had ideas for days but just never acted on them. I was successfully failing my university experience because of those habits. Then came September 11. That changed everything. Here I was thinking that this was the land of the free and I could continue living life as I was. In the early years came massive surveillance on our community. Somehow, I picked up on the surveillance because I observe things, as you know by now, and learn of things by trying to understand the process. Up until then I had been a procrastinator, failing in school and life. Thanks to my habits. I believed life was a journey and that one day I would know my purpose in life. We say in Africa, *Vunja mifupa kama bado meno iko*, literally meaning "break bones with teeth while you still can"—in essence, have fun in your youth while you can, before old age and responsibilities. I intended to have fun in my youth. When others were busy laying the foundations of their lives, I was busy smoking, partying, and chasing women. I was living the pursuit of l temporary happiness at the expense of long-term happiness and crossing the lines of my lord and religion. This always bothered me. I knew one day I would give up the habits, something all addicts tell themselves. Yeah, one day I will quit and put my life in order.

That day did not come for me until I realized I was under surveillance by the FBI. Somehow, I got labeled a potential threat, God forbid, a terrorist to be. Many get scared by this fact. I was not one of them, because I always believed that the enemy had no uniform but walks among us looking just like you and me. The enemy acts on their barbarity when it is too late. Think about this: the nineteen who attacked on September 11 had no criminal or antisocial behavior to warrant suspicion by some of the most sophisticated surveillance systems in the world. The FBI was just sorting people out, finding out who was trustworthy, who needed further checking, and more important, who deserved to be taken out of circulation.

My habits coupled with open surveillance. This was post-September 11. Our government, especially the FBI, was not even covert about it. They wanted it to be known, maybe as a tactic, maybe out of hubris, that we were under surveillance. This led me to a mental breakdown of bipolar disorder and paranoia of my surrounding. You see, distrust of someone leads to them distrusting their environment. As the years went by, the surveillance stayed on. At the beginning, it was heavy. Then came the age of informants, volunteers, and people-watchers. Basically, if you go to work, your colleagues keep tabs on you; go to school at the university and your fellow students keep tabs on you; go to any activity in public domain and the FBI itself keeps tabs on you. I did not mind at all, but it literally drove me nuts that I found myself in this position of distrust. I started questioning the process. At first, I said, "Why do they think I am a threat? Do they believe I am a terrorist? If not, why keep tabs on us so forcefully?" I knew I was good and doing good, harming none. But did they know that? Did they even care about us Muslims?

I did what I always do when curious. I learned about the FBI. I did my research on them. The FBI is an intelligence agency in charge of protecting America domestically. They were empowered by the USA PATRIOT Act with powers given by all Americans, Republicans and Democrats alike, bipartisan, to stop terrorism by any means necessary. This institution was one a lot was riding on. The pressure to stop another September 11 attack, unknown in scope, was tremendous. Congress, the public, and the media were baying for bodies and convictions of terrorists. At that time, you could say anything about Muslims and be believed. Paranoia was that of my country, my country was paranoid of us Muslims. We went bonkers and gave powers to an agency to do what it must do to stop the abomination of terrorism.

This surveillance led me to be so paranoid I lost my zest for life. Kept to myself, mostly, and a few friends were then recruited to keep tabs on me, so I cut off my friends too. I craved life pre-September 11, where I was not permanently suspected by an agency that believed I was a threat or, God forbid, a terrorist. The more I resisted, the more invasive the surveillance became. It was so pervasive that I reached a point of not even wanting to leave my house. I had a mental breakdown. Keep in mind that marijuana, khat, and alcohol played a role in it. "I think, therefore I am" is my philosophy in life. I did what I could and sought help to try to figure out how-to live-in society under permanent surveillance. I sought medical help. The thing is, under the PATRIOT Act, which later got renamed and slightly limited under President Obama as the USA Freedom Act, your doctor or psychiatrist does not have confidentiality or protections. Under that law, even your psychiatrist was part of the surveillance system, legally ordered to cooperate with and work for the FBI.

When I told them I was having difficulties with surveillance and the FBI, the psychiatrist diagnosed me as having a schizophrenic bi-polar disorder of hallucinations. Now, keep in mind, all psychiatrists in America, under law, are now an arm of the surveillance system. Here I was, working, doing activism, raising a family, paying my taxes, and being a good citizen. I do not believe psychiatrists meant me harm, but when one individual and a government agency hell-bent on secrecy and process get to decide, you get the idea as to who will be called crazy in America under national security paranoia. Trusting that they wanted to fully help me deal with my situation of psychosis based on open-ended surveillance was not an option. I cut off the psychiatrists but took their medicine to stop my mind from being overwhelmed by the surveillance process while trying to figure things out

Here I was, my privacy dead. I had none; people, coworkers, friends, some family, fellow students, and even at the mosque were keeping tabs on me, and they did not care what impact it was having on me mentally. Also, my psychiatrists were potentially an arm of the government surveillance system.

Paranoia set in, but I was determined to continue living free. I orchestrated an outlet. I would email my sisters my paranoid thoughts. I got on prescription drugs to deal with my bipolar disorder and stopped using marijuana. It was not meant for me. The doctor told me it height-

ens but does not cause paranoia. The effect on my mind was disastrous.
I quit it. Now you know why I claim I am a sinner. It came to a point
that even when going out on dates, I wondered how long it would be
before the FBI approached the lady to try keep more tabs on me.

In my research, I found out that we Muslims were not unique in being under surveillance by the FBI in its eighty-year history. In the early
stages of its formation, during the World War II, It was the Italians,
Germans, Swedes, Norwegians, Serbians, Japanese, Italians, and Irish
who were massively suspected of being enemy aliens and had to prove
their loyalty to America. The Japanese were even put into concentration
camps based on the paranoia of our government in America during
this time. Then came the Red Scare. It was the Jews turn. They were
considered communist sympathizers and got the treatment by the FBI.
This was in the 1950s. Then came the heyday of civil rights movements
and the leftist politics of antiwar movements. The left and black civil
rights leaders got the treatment by the FBI. The leftist, after outcries,
were left alone, but for the Black people this went on until the 1970s.
Ever heard of COINTELPRO? It was a program designed by the FBI
to make sure no black leader that they did not approve of emerged.
In essence, it was not about stopping harm to the country but about
population-control, specifically of black people in America. Then came
the world after September 11. Add the emergence of electronic means
beyond what could be imagined in previous times.

We Muslims are a minority in America—less than five million
people in this great country. I was black, Muslim, foreign-born and
politically opinionated, questioning things among friends and family
and online. Bingo. I hit the threat matrix. I was just a blue-collar worker
with no ambition. I had no criminal record, but then again, those that
did terrorism in America often didn't. Yep, I said to myself the original
sin. A young black man in America, Muslim in faith, foreign-born, not
native to the land, considered enemy alien. This surveillance was so
pervasive that I rebelled against it by any legal means I could. I pushed
back my way.

The first order of business was to profile my profilers, their approach mechanism, their informants, and to pick up what they thought of me. I learned to listen carefully. By now you know I base most of my knowledge on observing and reading. Again, open-source media was full of stories on how the FBI was doing its work against terrorism and they were effectively. Think about this: since September 11, no major terrorist attack has happened on American soil. You can thank the FBI for this because the terrorists are still trying. But in their explanation, using media, they would be leaking their operational details. They would tell the world exactly how they ensnared the culprit. This detailed bravado served me well to know exactly what would be coming my way under their surveillance system. The bad news is it does the same for the bad actors of the world. I always wondered how much money would be given to a coworker, friend, acquaintance, or just random person to set me up as a threat or terrorist or criminalize me one way or another. You live, you learn, was my attitude. Some of it was my paranoia, but I learned to sort out my paranoia, most of it, and to live in my newfound freedom.

Rule one was, if I have no privacy, I will post my life on social media. The FBI could not take by means of power what we freely give out to the world. In essence, I was the best informant on myself. I spoke truths, my truths, from political opinions to social opinions to the mundane, like my love of American football, go Vikings, always. Second, I was sending emails to my sister as a venting process. I knew my government read it. Hey, just in 2021, over three million Americans' emails were read by the FBI without a warrant. I would goad and push them, say something and watch how they reacted to it, the same thing they were doing to me under their permanent surveillance. What is good for the goose is good for the gander. I observed what elicited reactions and from whom. This was a basic science experiment. You put dye in an underground stream to see if the dye comes out in the river. All I had to do was listen and observe. I used it to profile their abilities, approach mechanism, methodology, and means of using information. More important, I profiled who they were using as informants. It worked like a charm.

I hated this surveillance for what it was doing to me. I was a man who had never hated anything. A live-and-let-live kind of guy who could rationalize anything until this point. I pushed and vented and pushed, privately, for years. This was using their format and means. They kept coming and coming and coming after me for it. They say the nail that stands out gets hammered. I was to be hammered into place. Now, I am an American, a proud Black man and a Muslim. I believed my place was anywhere I was accepted on the basis of merit and talents. To hell with affirmative action, just good old-fashioned merit-based criteria.

The second rule of my resistance: if my government and the FBI had me painted as a threat or, God forbid, a terrorist, when ISIS came to town in my beloved Minnesota, I said I would help them defeat it. Call me a violent person; I would show them the way of peace. Call me a threat; I would work earnestly to defeat the threats facing America. Call me a crazed man who needs to be watched; I would live life as best as I could according to my version of normal. In essence, I would push everything back to them to look again. Oh, this infuriated them. You see, the label of being a threat and terrorist is very profitable. It means work for informants, volunteers, agents, and surveillance. In essence, I represented budget-control and power. I learned this watching house hearings with FBI officialdom. I loved politics, and C-SPAN was the place to watch. Like I said, I was profiling the entirety of this agency to learn how to survive it. Every director will give a number; there are X amount of people we are very concerned about for their potential danger to society in America. I am sitting there in my house saying, yep, I am part of that X amount of people they are talking about. I am the reason they always ask for more budget, control, and power. I knew, and you know, and the FBI knew that I was not a threat or a terrorist. Once you are labeled, there is no coming back, just being worked on permanently until a suitable crime is found to get you out of circulation. The FBI was under the Beria age of doing things. Beria was the KGB head in the Bolshevik communist USSR. He told Stalin, the butcher of Russia and Eastern Europe, "Show me the man; I will show you the crime." The FBI labeled me a threat and worked diligently to create the crime to get me on by any legal means they could muster.

Let me be clear. This was not evil, this process, but it was a misguided use of our tax money and efforts as far as I was concerned. And I was a taxpayer and citizen of this great nation. I told you, I do things out of being selfish. If it does not serve the self, why do it at all? I am not one of those selfless people. I am kind and a gentleman, always, for the world is too hard to be so hard in outlook. I gave to charity until it hurt because I believed in expatiating my sins. I treat people with respect, give dignity, give alms, and always smile, laugh, and share joy and love into other people's hearts. This was not seen by the FBI. They saw their labeling system and their powers over us. That superseded everything in their understanding of what constituted their form of justice to us.

Two things happened while I was under surveillance. First my antics went up the chain. I call it the eating-popcorn effect. Powerful people across this country ate popcorn to see what was coming next. I was entertainment. It became evident that I would do anything within my rights, freedoms, and liberties to get the FBI to give back the rights, freedoms, and liberties they had appropriated. That meant the use of tools that exist for every American soul: Free speech, done privately over years, close to decades. Freedom to associate, to create means to help protect my country. It is taught by my faith, as in Christianity and Judaism, that for every bad you get, do good in return and your lord will reward you. I returned the favor for their distrust and surveillance by going to work, my way, of course going out and serving my country. This got me allies within the system in America. This got other agencies picking up on this fight for freedom by an Average Mohamed. Even international agencies picked up on it. I was the biggest open secret among my government as a subject of FBI surveillance. Heck, if I was entertainment, then I would do the jig to get them even more hooked.

It worked again like a charm. From the Department of Justice, the Department of Homeland Security, and the National Security Directorate all the way up to the White House, they knew of this Average Mohamed's battle with the FBI. This further infuriated the FBI system.

How do I know this? The surveillance went from being "let's watch him and keep tabs" to the FBI manipulating me to see what label they could fit me into and decide my destiny.

You see, the fact that they labeled us was proof of their system's god-like nature. I created a term for the system I found myself in: National Security Paranoia, when a government agency is hell-bent on proving we are threats and terrorists based on their analysis, which usually works for the good of country and saves lives. But in my instance, it was way off the mark. Then it is not national security anymore, but organized, biased paranoia on the taxpayer's dime and authority. We got into a measuring contest of wills. Average Mohamed will try get all his freedoms, rights, and liberties, and the FBI will infringe on them by any means necessary. The volunteers and informants were unleashed en masse on this Average Mohamed. It became a free-for-all fight. One man versus an institution. The popcorn-eaters kept watch and found this process to be entertainment. What will happen next? As if our lives were a soap opera and not those of free men and women in America. I will be honest; they tried, the others, to protect me, but the FBI gets who they want and target, always. The other powers mean nothing out here on the ground. Not even the President of the United States of America has powers to stop an FBI hell-bent on criminalizing an individual in America. The reason I profiled and came to understand was that this agency is not policed in checks and balances. In fact, it is the only agency in America that is not policed by any other entity. In essence, it runs like an independent government with no checks and balances. The local police department is policed by the city, the state, and the Department of Justice. Ask yourself this question: Who Polices the FBI? I did and guess what: it is only the FBI that polices the FBI. It's always an internal matter. Internally, I was considered a threat and now a crazy person.

Here I was in the freest country in the world, living like a East German communist under Stasi intelligence in the 1980s. I wanted no part in it, so I resisted this process by any legal means, privately, in my own way.

I went to work and created who I was: just an Average Mohamed in America. After all, I was a nobody, just a citizen, a regular dude who was a sinner too. I continued to live life, and when frustrated by the surveillance as it encroached further, I sent emails to my sister to vent and let go of my thoughts. This was all done privately for years. I pushed hard. The FBI pushed back harder.

Now, you would say, "Are you nuts, Mohamed?" The answer is, "Have you not understood one thing about what my cause and passion in life is?" *Freedom* for all against injustice, barbarity, and the powerful always getting one over on us. No exceptions and no exclusions of anybody. Just because we are nobodies does not mean we can't do anything. I am eternally an optimist; the light is just around the corner of this dark tunnel, is my attitude. This optimism says that good people can talk and come to an understanding. I kept on asking the FBI to talk in truths and end this chapter of the hostility of your agency against us. Power in secrecy and darkness, under National Security Paranoia, over Muslim activists is something they will never give up unless the cost is greater than what they gain. What they gain is power, budget, and control. I knew when I started profiling the FBI from top to bottom, from methodology to approach mechanisms, that there could be only one outcome: my destruction. But in the end, I will have achieved pushing the cause of freedom for all Americans one millimeter further in the future. I accepted that as payment. I wrote this book because I think it is vanity to hope another American will take up the resistance of National Security Paranoia.

I reached out formally to the Minneapolis FBI office and invited some agents to my house. I had met a few during my work engaging the community. You see, no matter my issue, they were still heroes who our democracy and republic needed to do their job to protect us all. I hated the terrorists whose actions gave our government the power to put blanket surveillance on my community. My focus publicly is going after the root cause terrorism, not the effect of surveillance. I will not mention names, but I brought two agents to my house, and we ate, and we spoke in generalities. I asked how I could be of service to the agency. I mean, we had just had the biggest ISIS case in America in my beloved Minnesota. They sponsored me to go through the FBI Citizens Academy, a three-month course on everything the FBI does. The Minneapolis FBI did that for me. I did what I had to do: doubled my medication for paranoia and went to the FBI building for three months to learn their perspective.

What I learned was revolutionary in nature. In my paranoia, all I could see was their surveillance. What I did not appreciate and came to learn was the true scope of their heroism in America. We went through case files. Each department head came to speak to us about everything from white-collar crime and corruption cases to counterintelligence in an age when dictators, theocrats, and communists were coming at America hard. I learned of the sex-crimes unit and how agents don't work there for long because of mental issues that affect them, the posttraumatic stress disorder that comes from the work of going after pedophiles. I learned of bomb-disposal team and how they protect America from domestic biological and nuclear attacks. I learned about the bank-robbery department, which has specialized in stopping it since the day of Al Capone. I learned of the firearms they use in their work. I learned that they're a diverse workforce of all peoples, sexualities, political affiliations, races, and identities. I learned of their communication team, which was my favorite, and how it talked in outreach into the community. Here I was, upset about surveillance but seeing firsthand the good surveillance does in stopping harm in America. I knew then this surveillance was not based just on prejudice, but that they had an evaluation system behind it. *Then why was their process so flawed that they came to my door?* I thought.

For a time, we had a honeymoon. I was shocked by how much our country needs them to just maintain law and order. What police could not do, they did. What transnational criminals, terrorists, spies, and pedophiles could do; they had the means to combat. They were in essence modern and very scientific in outlook. This was a revelation to me. Maybe I was wrong about them.

The surveillance continued unabated, though. Now, you would say at this junction, "This guy is paranoid." Yes, I am, but my paranoia is based on the surveillance system applied to me. I learned from profiling the FBI that I was not unique in this circumstance as a Muslim. A recent case in the Supreme Court is proof that what I say is very common. Imams who were put under surveillance despite the FBI publicly coming to their mosque and claiming they were not under surveillance sued the FBI with the American Civil Liberties Union. The case was *FBI v. Fazaga*. The Supreme Court ruled against Imams because—take a guess why. State secrets protection? In essence, National Security Paranoia against Muslims is protected by law. Just call it state secrets.

Trust in people named Mohamed is a very limited commodity in America. The surveillance made me paranoid and affected my pursuit of happiness. What I later discovered is that those who control your means of communication and keep tabs on your movement, even at work—well, they practically own you. Let me explain. We have given powers to the FBI in the belief they need these powers to stop harm from coming to America. Do they need these powers? I, for one, who gets death threats from violent jihadists, say, "Hell yeah, they do." The enemy is out there and coming for us all. But it also means those of us under surveillance are living under the pencil and eraser of a government agency to decide our destiny. What can we get, what are we allowed to do, who we can associate with, and what else is there, what opportunity we are allowed by the FBI in charge of maintaining the surveillance system? In essence your destiny is not yours to be decided as a citizen but is decided by FBI. I may be paranoid, but I saw over time my freedoms, rights, liberties and opportunities diminish. With the impact I was making, even the most ardent of haters within the FBI could not ignore me. Why, they had to work hard to stop Average Mohamed works. But here was a labeling agency that their superiors and other agencies came into the popcorn-eating-and-observing process of what of this Average Mohamed to whom we were budget, power, and control, and that further infuriated the agency that tripled down on their process. The more I pushed back, the more they pushed back, including psyops to make me unstable and push my paranoia even further into disfunction. In my profiling of the FBI, I learned that their modus operandi for me was different. I mean, I was and, at the writing of this book, still am free, but not completely free or even an equal in America. That was not about my race; black folks came after me the hardest about my religion, the chosen few, and the new Jim Crow system under National Security Paranoia. In essence, who becomes a leader or activist in our community is being decided, most are leftists and democrats who get accepted by the FBI as community leaders. Look into all the Muslim organizations they gave an award to in the past twenty years in Minnesota and then look at what Republican-leaning activists and Muslims like Average Mohamed are getting. A substantial amount of our community is in the informants' ranks, working to protect our country, and being foreign-born Somali did not help my cause, because the hierarchy is like a mountain of nativists. I was also a known Republican activist, and if you now watch polls, the Republicans are soured on the agency because of bias against them for good reason: the agency is becoming more and more openly partisan. People are not stupid; they can see it in America clearly. Half the country today has serious reservations about the FBI. They just don't trust them anymore—mostly Muslims, a minority of five million people, and Republicans, whom it is now open season on for the FBI, just like with us Muslims.

I learned that first comes the label "threat" or "terrorist," God forbid. Then comes the distrust implemented by surveillance from home, car, and work to places like university and mosque. The infrastructure is thrown at you to keep tabs on you. When you question the reasoning behind this, they will deny it is even happening. They think we are all stupid not to see it. Call it state secrets and wave around nondisclosure agreements like scarlet letters or just put fear into people. Most people are decent; they just say yes, as they would help their country. The public-health impact of surveillance is so pervasive in my Somali Muslim community that we have a word, *buufis*, meaning folks who end up mentally ill because of it. Like I was.

Then comes the discounting. He can't do that, he is not well enough, he doesn't eat well to keep up his health, he does not take his prescriptions, he is not capable of being a counter-ideologist. The naysaying is permanent and entrenched in the system. I just watched and observed based on how they were treating me.

Then comes the denial, the whisper campaign done off-the-books. That means no matter how many grants I write, how many networks I reach out to do more work in defeating hate, fighting extremism, and promoting democracy, there is an agency, the FBI, with a pencil and an eraser over my life. I am blacklisted by the FBI in America, though it is hard to prove it. But I have been on the covers of *The Wall Street Journal*, *Star Tribune*, and *USA Today*. I have awards from esteemed organizations, nationally and internationally. I have done works in schools, mosques, madrassa, synagogues, churches, and even civic arenas. Yet I can't get networks established, and everything goes through what I now call the Monkey Wrench Process. You throw a monkey wrench into a moving machine to stop it or slow it down. You see, from their labelling, I learned to label their activities around me too. What's good for the goose is good for the gander. I profiled my profilers to know that the whisper campaign is permanent phase of surveillance. I go to political events; they are there, and then folks turn around and say, "OK, why are you here?" I go to meetings and folks go from being excited, wanting to build things and do works together, to silence on the next matter. Just silence, mostly—some are decent enough to reply, "I am busy" or "We don't have funds for it." The permanent whisper campaign ensures we don't do anything to go beyond their labels. Again, we are budget, power, and a means of control, not free men or women anymore, once the FBI puts you under surveillance and in its crosshair. Plus, who the hell are these others, powerful enough to tell the FBI leave me be? No matter how powerful they were to make them pause internally, the only reason I am free is that I have protectors within our awesome government. Folks who love our work and want it but will not go against the FBI in their analysis and whisper campaign. Well, it is done out of sight but persistently. "To what purpose is this all being done?" I ask, and that enrages folks even more internally. These folks do not believe in accountability of their powers. This was done privately in the venting process of sending emails.

The Monkey Wrench Process served two purposes. First, to discourage their efforts; again, my destiny was being decided by an agency. "If we, the FBI, put up enough roadblocks and pressure to make things never go right, consistently and permanently, he will give up." Those who control your communication from emails to phones and electronically leash you, well, they can do that every day. The second is a psyop leading to the buildup of frustrations that clog our mind and cause a mental breakdown. This they all knew because, like I said, they also have psychiatrists figuring out how to push us to make us malleable to their labels, such as "He is crazy." I agree I am bipolar as a direct result of FBI surveillance. It did not exist as a psychosis prior to surveillance. "Even then, when did one in four Americans suffering from mental illness become national security threats?" I asked the FBI. "Is this now the FBI policy in America?" If it is, they need to come out in the open with it.

I questioned and challenged and pushed back my way, by keeping an optimistic attitude. I came upon my other means of resistance: if the doors are shut, come through the chimney like Santa Claus. I snuck through the chimney into media and activism and was allowed to get small grants, but every big idea I had was shut down. Every major association for big projects backed out, one by one by one, systematically, like clockwork, from the Monkey Wrench Process of being blacklisted by the FBI. The doors were slammed shut by the FBI, but they left the chimney open, and if a fat, jolly, red-hat-wearing white guy can do it, so can an Average Mohamed. If Santa brought gifts, so did this Average Mohamed to democracies and republics for the cause of freedom. But I did not get the customary cookies and milk. I got more surveillance and the Monkey Wrench Process.

What end does this surveillance serve? Well, it is not all bad, and I already told you of my outlook that if you are good and do good, you have nothing to worry about. This agency is not evil; they are heroes, but we are out here going at it with labels and resistance actions and counter-reactions. My brother said, "If you ever compete with elephants in shitting, your rear will tear." I was one man, an Average Mohamed, and they were an institution with, it seems, volunteers coming out of the woodwork to come at me mentally or get me to do things they wanted. To monkey wrench my processes and create psyops to keep me unstable mentally. The purpose, I have come to conclude, is to discard me and my activism.

Let me explain. You are not put under surveillance because you are a saint. This is an investigation process. The FBI does not come into your work, electronically leashes you, surveillance your phone, home, car, and social settings to just to get to know you. They do it because they have reasonable worries that you are a threat, in my case a terrorist. The endgame is to discard who they suspect to be a threat. That is their job. I have nothing against their job in general, but when it comes to my case, I have everything against it. How could an agency get it so wrong and then triple down on their process? Even when they knew how wrong they were, off-the-books and on? Well, I did question them hard and pushed back by resistance. That does not make friends of those working on the ground in the FBI or their leadership. I had honor, decency, and respect. I told them about what I was doing, and my goal was *freedom* from them and their surveillance. I did get some form of protection from others within the system, but because of the blue wall of silence, the FBI will look the other way as others use extrajudicial means like whisper campaigns and the Monkey Wrench Process.

The last part is to destroy. To get me out of circulation, one way or another at this juncture. To criminalize me under one law or another. I had not made enemy of my country but was now a known enemy of the agency because I would not give up an inch of my rights, liberties, freedoms, and opportunity. I am no threat or terrorist come whatever outcome.

The volunteers pushed back even harder. They even told me their name, years back; they called themselves Bust a Nut Crew. I was the nut to be busted by the volunteers constantly coming after me in ways agents could not. Now asymmetrical threats were coming my way. "Your family will be targeted, all of them, and squeezed by us. If you ever go back to Africa or travel anywhere, we will get you there." At this juncture, we had reached the breaking point of our process. I asked for years for a direct dialogue to end this chapter, and they came with their terms. You see, had the FBI asked me, I would have willingly given them what they wanted because I believe most of them are heroes. But I react to force and power the same way I reacted against violent jihadists. Smile, laugh, have joy and love in my heart for them but go against them in efforts. Push back.

My rear is about to tear right about now. That is why I wrote this book, in the vanity that you all can put your mettle and support behind an Average Mohamed in the public realm and shit back with me, for an institution, the FBI, is shitting on me constantly, and I cannot keep up at this time, for they are an institution, and I am one man. I need other men and women, citizens, to help me shit back. This is a shitstorm we find ourselves under. I need allies and friends in this cause. I don't mind prison, as you know by now. If I did not mind violent jihadist death threats, why should I be afraid of the place they, the FBI, have sent other civil rights leaders? Plus, I will not only survive but thrive in there, adapt and do more works, like writing my second and third books, memorizing the Quran, and getting a master's degree or even a PhD depending on the time I'm given in prison. If I end up dead by the asymmetrical means of the Bust a Nut Crew volunteers because I know the level of hate coming at me, then it was ordained. Why worry about what I have no control over?

I asked the FBI for years to either come to terms or come get me so that we may formally fight it out in the public. The answer to this question, which was heard by so many, including all the agencies of America, was silence and a quadrupling of the FBI process. What I now call the velvet glove on our throat. The throat is the channel that we eat and nourish ourselves and breathe through. Put your hand on it; you can restrict it. The FBI put on a velvet glove and tripled their psyops to use my mental illness against me. The Monkey Wrench Process was heightened, and all this was done to say, "Look, he can't function; he is crazy; therefore, a new threat matrix evolves to get him out of the way." More labels, more budget, more power, and control.

Average Mohamed

The national security paranoia response to their citizen, out here helping them win this war, is silence and more means of coercion and surveillance. More volunteers, more analysis by shrinks, more evaluations, and more of the same shit as before. The honor, respect, and dignity of my silence, even when the media was calling me from across the world, had no meaning to them in an age when everyone is outraged and running to media for outlet. I had no value to them but as an eternal punching bag to keep hitting until they break me, one way or another. I was a nobody to an agency that even Reverend Martin Luther King Jr. could not escape. Those who survived being targeted by the FBI did so by leaving the country in exile. Then there were those that stayed, like Oppenheimer, the scientist who created the atom bomb, who became a peace activist. Lenny Bruce, the comedian who skirted social norms, got destroyed. I mean even Trump, from day one, was being targeted, but he does himself no favors. The reason why I voted for him twice was not his politics. God help me, his politics were populist nationalism, and that turned me off. I prefer more sober means. The reason why I voted for him was because, like me, he was a fighter in a losing cause. Like they did to me, they came at him from every angle, and like me, he fights back. I could relate to that about him. That meant something to me. Apparently seventy-nine million Americans agree with that statement. Today the FBI calls them thanks to their need for more budget and power to control insurrectionists, domestic terrorists, and subversives. Some do exist, but Republicans are now getting it like I am. And I am a Republican activist, too, so I get it at twice their level.

I knew at the beginning of this process of resistance and questioning authority that changing my status was doomed, based on the history of eighty years of this agency. "A leopard does not change its spots," is an African saying. This is the legacy of J. Edgar Hoover, and we gave the FBI great, unchecked powers, which they need to secure America. That even I will not go against, for at the end of the day, why would I do all my works if not for the protection of my family, country, and humanity? Why should I hate to say, as folks on the right now do, "Defund the FBI?" That is just nuts. We need the FBI for our national security, but we need them to be professional and without National Security Paranoia when the facts emerge otherwise. But far-right thinking is angry and partisan now. Anger never solved a problem; it just compounds it, as I tell my Republican friends. This agency has heroes even though it's gone partisan now. We still have time to correct it, but defund it? This is going so far right you end up on the left, like shouting, "Defund the police!" What did we get out of defunding police in America but more crime in all our cities? What we will get out of defunding the FBI is a national security disaster. I will not go there, because I honor, dignify, and respect this agency but don't mind now publicly coming out and saying "you went wrong here" in analysis and labeling an Average Mohamed in America, no matter the consequences to me. The fact I am writing this—and they are reading it as I do—and I am still free is a testament that they are not evil but can be wrong occasionally. I will get destroyed, but my message about who led this process—the FBI— and why will be heard. I will not run, hide, or give up, ever; that is the American way. I will push the cause of freedom one millimeter in America by these writings.

For the Republican side of America, I want to tell you what black people told us Muslims after September 11, "You are the new Blacks in America." We Muslims are now telling you, "You are the new Muslims in America." This process of labeling and works done to this Average Mohamed I was just a pioneer for this age of yours all. These folks are perfecting it for you. Some of the Republican bases are straight domestic terrorists, and they need to be cleared out. Just like some Democrats, like antifa, are the same. Average Mohamed works against both sides to stop extremism in America. No exception, no exclusion. Though the rhetoric of our government, media, and public, you hear the same stuff about Republicans that they said about Muslims. Yep, Republicans are the new Muslims now. If I got this treatment, some undeserving Republicans shall get it too. You are over a hundred million; just like the left got the FBI off their backs in the 1970s, you will need to organize to get the same effect. But Republicans must be honest and brave enough to go after domestic terrorists too to get there.

As an idealist, I propose a bill of rights for those under surveillance. If I know I am under surveillance, is there an ombudsman I can go to get out from under it? Is there an agency or person in our government that can say, "Look at this process of the FBI?" After George Floyd was martyred, we did this for all police departments in America. Should we not be doing the same for this federal agency?

In essence, we need to bring people's power back into the FBI processes. We need them checked and balanced democratically by us, the people, for the people, by the people. We need a bill of rights that says destiny is the domain of the surveilled. That the powers vested in an agency are to be used solely to stop criminality and terrorism, not for an open-ended inquisition to confer labels, not creating terrorists and criminals by other means, starting with labeling. Definitely not a return to their COINTELPRO ways for Muslims and now, Republicans, of population suppression of activists and citizens. In other words, do not manufacture enemies where none exist, like Average Mohamed. No matter their needs for budget, power, and control, here I am, fighting and getting death threats from jihadists, dealing with hate mail, cancel culture, and an open-ended phishing expedition over multiple years of surveillance by the FBI, their volunteers, unleashed off-the-books, and informants, a loose coalition calling itself Bust a Nut Crew. I cannot travel back home to Africa until this issue comes out publicly. I also am coming out for my family. I fear what comes next to my large extended family, here and in Africa, from the volunteers and informants.

I learned one true value from all the communities I have mentioned that got the same treatment of mistrust in America. Be true to America, and in time she shall be true to you. Do not pull an Anwar al-Awlaki, a prolific nemesis and opposite of this Average Mohamed and the best recruiter of English-speaking violent jihadists. He was in America, a citizen of the greatest nation on earth, and the FBI knew of his habits and suspected he was a threat because of previous associations. They confronted him with his habit of prostitution engagement as an imam. He balked ran to back to his ancestral land, Yemen, where he was promptly arrested, did time, hooked up with al-Qaeda, and began a propagating violent jihad so well that he was personally responsible for thousands of young, English-speaking Muslims joining violent jihad. He was killed in a drone strike. Anwar al-Awlaki was a national security threat, but he got no jury or judge to convict him. He was killed by an executive order from our government. Even after death, his ideas are working around the world. Therefore, I created Average Mohamed to counter him, Jihadi John, and others in messaging. My role in life and destiny is to destroy that ideology, and I am considered one of the best in the world at it. Anwar al-Awlaki was not true to America. If my government had pictures of me and with prostitute or in promiscuity, I would want copies of it for myself. I would tell them, "Is that all you got from your surveillance?" and remain true to America. It is a mindset that says no matter your circumstances, this is by far the greatest country in the world, one in which I am proudly an American. Period. I will not turn on it despite the massive effort by the FBI to make us into threats of our great country. Anwar al-Awlaki forgot America is freedom. Average Mohamed will never do that, no matter the circumstances or efforts by the FBI and their unleashed volunteers and informants, Bust a Nut Crew. My work speaks volumes on this fact.

The only reason I come out now in public is because I fear harm coming my way or to my family here and abroad through off-the-books means. I asked persistently to end this process and made enemies of rank-and-file folks all the way to leadership of the FBI. Officially and in front of protectors, all is kosher and halal. But out here there is hate for Average Mohamed based on my questioning of this blanket authority that came into my life. Why teach us immigrants the values of America, to question authority, and get mad with hate when we do so? The FBI is an institution of heroes, but they looked at evil for so long they forgot what good looks like. It is also our job to show good to them too. To dissent is patriotic. It's dangerous and foolish for Muslims in the post-9/11 world and for Republicans after the January 6 insurrection against National Security Paranoia. But you just got to love America. Even here, we can have limited freedoms, rights, and liberties to speak out. Here we have freedom of speech, freedom to associate, freedom of thought, and the rights of kings. They were given to us by millions who bled, marched, protested, lobbied, and voted. We are not going to give it up to the FBI easily. Average Mohamed, in the tradition of those nameless folks, is not about to give up rights, freedoms, and liberty, hard-won from the powerful, no matter the consequences.

Did I say anything seditious? To some within the agency, this gives me a new label and threat index. The labeling system goes on no matter the means of resistance to deny, discount, discourage, discard, and destroy. I had honor, respect, and dignity for their authority and told them I would be doing this, coming out in public today, on my birthday, as I write this book. We seek freedom, liberty, rights, equal opportunity, and access to resources in equity and inclusion. Even that is sedition today, according to some out here who believe they have an eraser and pencil over our lives.

I simply say, "No." Destiny is the domain of the citizen, not our government, with all due respect to authority in our democracy and republic, the United States of America. With all our dignity and might, we will simply resist the powerful from getting over us with their power when they are wrong. I asked politely, peacefully, and nonviolently for reconciliation and got rejected, and the process accelerated, publicly and secretly, which is why I wrote this book. An exercise in vanity to pass on the message, "Support the FBI when it's doing good but hold it accountable when it errs in its ways." National Security Paranoia has got to go, for me, for Muslims, and for Republicans, by all legal and necessary means. The words of Malcolm X remain true. "Anytime you beg another man to set you free, you will never be free. Freedom is something that you must do for yourselves."

This chapter is dedicated to all our freedoms, rights, liberty, opportunities, and pursuit of happiness. The issue is inclusion and equity from the powerful. Damn the consequences.

Chapter 10
What Next?

Continue with Average Mohamed Works, Expanding to After-School Programs

What is next for the Average Mohamed organization? We are working on even more cartoons. We have more ideas than resources. A series of collections we want to create will tackle antisemitism, racism, Islamo-phobia, anti-LGBTQI+, and anti-Christianity. You can see a sample, the first of the series, on the Average Mohamed YouTube page. Please subscribe to it as we continuously update it.

Hate is unacceptable anywhere in our republic and democracy. We should be prepared to counter its pervasive, ever-changing nature on social media, internet, and in the public domain. Now it's popping up on video games and consoles. I will speak up against it in articles, speeches, and engagements in schools, mosques, madrassa, synagogues, churches, and even civic arenas. I will create more if I can get more resources. It cost me only three cents to reach a soul on social media. Facebook, or Meta, is helping our process, giving us free credits. We hope to add YouTube and others to the cause. I believe in free social media sites that can help us all in this process of defeating extremism and hate and promoting democracy. We have written papers about this, available on my website, www.averagemohamed.org. We have been researched in papers by the University of Southern California, the RAND Corporation, the Institute for Strategic Dialogue, and others, and received a special mention from the United Nations Development Program. We will welcome researchers to our data and analytics to further our understanding and perfect our works.

We want to visit Africa, Asia, and the Middle East if we can get resources and equal opportunity to train activists, clergy, influencers, governments, and especially women leaders who reached out and want our program, methodology, and process for themselves and their countries, whom I have a long list of. I can't get resources, being blacklisted by the FBI, but when I can—and I have applied for so many opportunities, domestically and internationally—I will. What we seek is to teach the basics of the process from messaging criteria to dissemination. What took me eight years to learn, we can pack into three weeks of teaching. I dream of creating over a one thousand Average Mohamed's, Average Ariels, Average Jose's, Average Joes, Average Mary's, Average Aisha's, and many more to do what we do. The ideas are there, but like me, they face obstacles to resources. We must convince our government that the hammer and ears on the ground are needed, but counternarratives that can win minds are more important to save the next generation from the pipeline of hate and extremism. This is the key to the survival of our diversity, plurality, and freedoms in the long run. This is also something I am personally going to go lobby Congress on in the future.

Average Mohamed hooked up with an African media company to create realistic puppets in a show called *Kaftan Show* for Somalia, which means "jokes show," a rip-off of *Saturday Night Live* making fun of al-Shabab, politicians, and stars of the republic in the promotion of democracy, rights, liberties, and freedoms for the democratic, secular, rising Somali republic. I applied for resources and paid for the pilot myself. I am still paying for process myself nine years later. I don't mind at this juncture of life. The work must go on; we decide our destiny in America. Even if the FBI is planning our destiny, we make our plans, and our Lord is the best of planners.

We applied with our government to go back into schools, this time with a program meant to deal with violence, teaching nonviolence and peaceful means. We partnered with many organizations to do so.

We wish to open an after-school program to get kids to use their ideas, as we have worked in the past with the Saint Paul Police Department and the Metropolitan Regional Arts Council in direct engagement in the Twin Cities, based on its curricula and format.

Average Mohamed is seeking expertise to create a curriculum from existing products tailored for schools: a work-study program for our youths across the world, especially for American kids. We need networks and resources to deliver it. You already know why that is impossible to achieve under National Security Paranoia.

Going into Business Again: Mossa Samosa

On a personal level, I opened a new venture, a food manufacturing company called Mossa Samosa. Samosa, also called *sambuusa* and other names, is an Indian food that is also eaten in the Middle East and Africa. We are manufacturing it for retail stores in packages for refrigerators. It's a new type of samosa, an Americanized version of a staple of Africa, the Middle East, and Asia. We are baking it instead of deep frying it. A samosa is a wrap of flour with either meat filling, vegetable, or both. I have finalized this process after months of research and development, spending, God help me, tens of thousands in the process to have 90 percent less fat than a regular samosa. Hence a Mossa Samosa. Mossa is my brother, who is the lucky charm in my family. Plus, it rhymes.

Our Mossa Samosa also includes a first for its kind: it has cheese in it. Heck, we are in Midwestern cheese country out here in Minnesota. We put cheese into everything. I created and taste-tested the product to be for the American palate. They say it tastes just like a burger without the fat. I am creating a mainstream American snack. One thing all can agree on is the democratization of food. We eat all regions' food in America. Why not a Mossa Samosa too? *Inshallah*, if God wills it, we should have all the licenses to sell across America, online and at retail stores, by the early 2023. I love this part, for I did not hide the fact that I am an avowed capitalist. Making a buck is equivalent to the greatest rush one can get and satisfying when one can make a living from it.

Wish me luck on this venture, for it costs a quarter-million to go from concept to stores with a food product. Most food companies do not last one year from their formation date. The competition is tough, as samosas already exist in the market. Mine is a Mossa Samosa, coming to a store near you if God will it. You can also buy it online; google "Mossa Samosa." Hey, I would not be a capitalist if I did not ask you to buy the product and sell it too if you are a retailer. Enjoy a good, American-made, USDA-approved snack with meat, flour, and cheese.

Baby Five on the Way—Time for Family Too

On the family side, I had baby number five—a boy, who came in healthy. I named him Zayn, meaning grace, in praise of our lord who is grace to me in bounties like a child. For we are all those in need of grace. I am going for six kids. My Mormon fiends in Utah and orthodox Jews understand what I mean. But an American sensibility says, why? We are here by science to pass our genes, by religion to worship God, and by the republic to be taxpayers. The more that procreate, the merrier. I love my kids more than anything except my mom—yep, mama's boy. I am excited about it. I already have three daughters and son. *Inshallah*, after this, one more to go. We are here to procreate and advance our humanity. Each child is expensive, but they come with their blessings. Each is unique, a budding human being. It is just a joy to see them develop into little people, and now I have teenagers. Americanized teenagers who are as free-spirited and opinionated as me, smart as hell and ambitious in education and religion, all of them learning to memorize the Quran by age fifteen and many other things. This is my true wealth in this world. My true legacy. Works and passions and money, these are transient. Even freedom, I learned, is temporary. But family binds.

My father passed away this year, may he see our noble Prophet Mohammad in heaven and be given his book of life in the right hand. My extended family is growing and thriving across the world. We are the new nomads of the world. The Somali people's ways still live, making a home and building societies wherever we lay our heads for the duration of our lives.

Going Back to Basics

I want to revert to Islam and be a better Muslim, keeping to *dhikr* and prayers. I do thousands a day. But the soul is weak. I pray for myself, parents, family, kinfolks, tribe, people, country, and humanity all the time. I feel it is free to pray; why be a miser about it and be selective; why not pray for all? *Inshallah*, a sinner will find his way back. I think I am almost there now, with age and perspective. Going back to basics, the greatest inheritance I got from my parents is Islam. I want to be a better father and *mu'min*, or believer. I chant all day and night and pray all the time. It helps my mental well-being to praise and venerate my Lord. I hope it saves my soul from eternal hell.

The subclan and tribe I belong to have asked me to do something for them, to bring opportunities back to Somalia, Puntland, Eyl. I have a project I am working on to bring one thousand jobs to the tribes in a cooperative self-ownership program. I have done the research and analytics for a profitable venture that they will, *inshallah*, fund at a $1000 buy-in for shares, hoping to raise a capital. This will be owned by the people, for the people, and for their economic gain. I am working with venture capitalists, aid groups, and others to make this happen, *inshallah*, in the coming years.

Scaling Up Ambitions in Languages, Trainings, and Outreach

We are here to tire our mind, body, and soul, I believe as a square, and as you have read, I live a very purposeful life. We came a long way to claim being Americans as immigrants. America is a promise to us immigrants. If we can work hard, innovate, have positive spirits, and then work even harder, we can at least get our American dream. The American dream is one predicated on equal opportunity and access to resources in equity and inclusion. I can achieve, as so many immigrants to America the great of past generations have. The natives taught me this, and I teach in values and works that it is still a reality in America.

Now, I should be sour on America. Damn the government and this system. Call it systemic racism, Islamophobia, nativist haters of foreign-born Americans out to get mentally ill folks and Republicans. But that would be a false analogy. Instead, I choose to say America is the greatest country, where, if you can dream, you can get your dream. Where even if you dissent, you don't end up dead or in jail, hopefully, as has been true in the past, even when facing our government or an agency of it. Where an Average Mohamed can work for his republic and democracy and be embraced by the state department and Global Ties with awards. Where I get to speak my piece everywhere, even though my opinions and politics are known publicly. Where one can do business and create a future of profitability with help from mentors from corporations to banks to investors. Where the people, although divided and very politically tribal and partisan today—donkeys and elephants, Democrats and Republicans—have more in common than we disagree on. America is the last bastion of freedom in this world. We lose America and its way and freedom dims in this world. Democracy is messy, and it sucks compared to the order of communism, dictatorship, and theocracy, the iron-fisted ways of suppressing people's spirits. But it is the best humanity has come up with for people to have actual power over the strong. Not all power to the elite and powerful, who we need, but we have leverage too. We have freedoms that give us the rights of kings and queens, and we have the opportunity, when unmolested, to be all we can be.

In this country, if you are true to it and its ideals, one can go very far in development and achievements. As a black man, a Muslim, a foreign-born bipolar person and a proud Republican, I claim to be an American. There is more good here than bad. That does not mean we don't tackle the bad.

The lesson I've learned living here for almost twenty-seven years is to believe in America. If not you, despite your conditions and circumstances, whether they be good or bad, who will believe in America?

We just need the equal opportunity, access to resources, and equity and inclusion to deliver on all this. I need the FBI off my back—to have my back, as they are supposed to. But more and more Americans, in fact, half this country in a recent poll, feel the FBI is on our backs. That needs to change, and I am coming out publicly to push for that after privately being denied, discounted, discredited, discarded, and fearing to be destroyed.

Why do our works as Average Mohamed?

We are the new age *freedom fighters* of the world. We will fight for freedom, liberties, justice, equality, and opportunity for all to pursue their happiness. No exception, no exclusion, globally. We will do so peacefully and nonviolently as true revolutionaries of freedom for all humanity. People's power. That is what the natives taught me, the immigrant, and now I am teaching it to the world.

I tell you; it feels good to be an American.

Here we choose to live, for life is worth living, and if we are going to live it, we choose to live it *free*. Free from hate and extremism, free to promote our democracy, free in rights and liberties, not just for us but against the dictatorships, communists, and theocrats of the world.

Our Average Mohamed works.

We stand for the good in this world. We, you, and I together, as *freedom fighters today.*

When the average people can dream and go to work, nothing is impossible, like Nelson Mandela taught us all. "It is impossible until it is done." If I can do it, so can you. Power to the people in peace and nonviolent ways. For it takes an idea to defeat the ideas harming humanity. One message at a time, one soul at a time.

Our Average Mohamed works.

Lightning Source UK Ltd.
Milton Keynes UK
UKHW010818090223
416681UK00002B/395